Classic
Chain Mail
Jewelry
WITH A TWIST

SUE RIPSCH

KALMBACH BOOKS

Kalmbach Books
21027 Crossroads Circle
Waukesha, Wisconsin 53186
www.Kalmbach.com/Books

Published in 2013
17 16 15 14 13   2 3 4 5 6

Manufactured in the United States of America

ISBN: 978-0-87116-483-4
EISBN: 978-0-87116-756-9

Editor: Erica Swanson
Art Director: Lisa Bergman
Layout Artist: Rebecca Markstein
Photographer: William Zuback, James Forbes

Library of Congress Cataloging-in-Publication Data
Ripsch, Sue.
  Classic chain mail jewelry with a twist / Sue Ripsch.

    p. : col. ill. ; cm.

    Issued also as an ebook.
    ISBN: 978-0-87116-483-4

  1. Jewelry making--Handbooks, manuals, etc. 2. Chains (Jewelry)--Handbooks, manuals, etc. 3. Chains (Jewelry)--Patterns. 4. Metal-work--Handbooks, manuals, etc. I. Title.

TT212 .R572 2013
745.594/2

Contents

Introduction

Welcome to my second book featuring the wonderful jewelry-making technique known as chain mail. I hope *Classic Chain Mail Jewelry with a Twist* will be a major addition to your chain mail library, and I worked to make each piece beautiful and unique. Illustrated instructions with newly added rings shown in blue are designated for the beginner, intermediate, and advanced jewelry maker. It can be great fun to challenge yourself by making increasingly more difficult weaves, and this book will offer the reward for your efforts with timeless chain mail jewelry that you will wear for years.

Silver-filled metal has made silver jewelry more affordable, and I'll share a bit of information about rings made from this metal. I will also include a description of the process for making your own jump rings. The method of making jump rings is important, as high-quality and well-made jump rings translate into sturdy, professional jewelry.

Caring for your jewelry can be as important as the process for making it. You'll find information in this book about tumbling (sometimes called polishing) jump rings, as well as finishing whole jewelry pieces.

For even more design possibilities, aspiring chain mail artists play with weaves using the concept of aspect ratio. In a nutshell, the aspect ratio is a mathematical calculation that you can use to change the scale of a piece of jewelry. For instance, with the aspect ratio, you can take a petite bracelet and give it more presence or heft with jump rings of a different gauge and inner diameter than in the original piece.

In my first book, *Classic Chain Mail Jewelry*, I shared information about the history of chain mail, metals used for the jewelry, technical details concerning jump ring gauge and sizes, tools used with the technique, storage of jump rings, and work area considerations. You can refer to that book for a review of basic chain mail making, if needed.

Finally, note that not all of the weaves in this book are original to me, but the instructions are my own. I hope that you will find this book to be a true building block.

Sue Ripsch

Basics
MAKING JUMP RINGS

If you are in need of a refresher, please refer to my first book, *Classic Chain Mail Jewelry*. The information in this section goes the next step beyond the basics.

SILVER-FILLED JUMP RINGS

In *Classic Chain Mail Jewelry*, I discussed different metals that have been used to make jump rings for use in chain mail jewelry. Since then, the market has seen a surge in the price of gold, and this has caused the silver market to rise dramatically as well.

Gold-filled wire has long been available to make jump rings that are gold on the outside with an alloy in the center. Think of a garden hose that is made of gold, and the water running through the hose is an alloy. This is what gold-filled rings are:

a hollow tube of gold with an alloy in the center. These rings are less expensive than jump rings made of solid gold.

Now, the silver market has followed suit. Silver-filled wire is now available for making jump rings. The cost of silver-filled rings is approximately 40 percent less than that of sterling silver rings. I have made and worn jewelry made of silver-filled rings, and the rings look like sterling silver and, to date, seem to wear like it as well. This material offers an affordable alternative to more-expensive metals.

BASIC OR SIMPLE METHOD

To make a jump ring, start with wire. Jump rings are sized in two dimensions, which are gauge and inner diameter (ID). To give the jump ring the correct ID, you wrap the wire around a rod that is the size of the specific ID that you want the ring to have. The rod can be a wooden dowel, a metal rod, a knitting needle, or anything else that is the correct size. Once you have the gauge of wire and the rod in the ID that you want, hand wrap the wire around the rod into a coil. There are also motorized methods of winding a coil. This wound coil will be cut and become your jump rings.

To cut the rings, you will need a few extra materials: a jeweler's vise, a jeweler's saw, saw blade lubricant, a bench pin (optional), and a wooden dowel for support. The jeweler's equipment and saw blade lubricant can be purchased at jewelry supply stores or online at jewelry supply sites.

A jeweler's vise has jaws that have removable rubber protective inserts that help avoid marring the metal. A jeweler's saw has special blades that are made of high-quality tool steel and are very flexible. You want a high-quality, flexible blade that has very sharp teeth along the edge.

To cut the coil, first coat the saw blade with a saw blade lubricant that helps keep the blade cool (lubricant will also help prolong the life of the blade).

For rings that will have an ID of 6.5mm or greater, place a wooden dowel in the center of the coil when you are cutting it. The dowel does not have to be the exact ID that the coil was made for. It may be smaller, as this dowel only offers support during the cutting process. For rings with IDs smaller than 6.5mm, you can cut the coil without the additional support of a dowel.

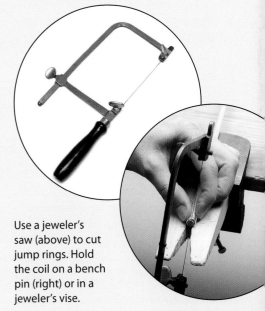

Use a jeweler's saw (above) to cut jump rings. Hold the coil on a bench pin (right) or in a jeweler's vise.

Tighten the coil in the vise or place on a bench pin, and cut a straight line with the jeweler's saw along the length of the coil. This makes the coil into individual jump rings. Tumble-polish the rings (p. 7).

Basics
MAKING JUMP RINGS

Helpful Hints

- When using the jeweler's saw, be sure that the blade is fastened tightly within the saw frame. Be sure not to overtighten the blade, or it will break. Likewise, you do not want the blade to be too loose, or it will not cut properly.
- Place and keep the saw frame perpendicular to the coil throughout the cutting process if using a bench pin.
- When using a jeweler's vise, saw the coil, use long, even strokes, drawing the blade across the whole length of the coil as you work. It is important to cut the entire coil at once instead of stopping and starting.

Professional Jump Ring Maker Method

Professional jump ring makers are pieces of equipment used to wind and cut jump rings. They are made by many manufacturers and come in a broad range of prices. A jump ring maker helps you to form a more uniform diameter ring and aids in making clean, straight cuts. This is important because then the two ends of the jump ring will close together smoothly and tightly for your piece of jewelry. A professional system comes with metal mandrels in

popular diameters. The less-expensive systems will require you to hand-wrap the wire into a coil as described earlier. The more expensive systems include a motorized method of winding the wire into a coil.

To make rings with a professional jump ring maker system, begin with wire in the gauge that you desire and a mandrel that is the diameter for your finished rings. When winding rings into a coil for the motorized method, place the correct-sized metal mandrel in the chuck of a drill motor to power-wind the wire. Once the chuck is tightened, place the wire through the hole in the mandrel to begin winding. If there is no hole in the mandrel, place the end of the wire in the opening between jaws of the chuck. As you run the drill, feed the wire at a 90-degree angle to the length of the mandrel. Be sure to keep uniform tension on the wire while the coil is forming. It is important to wind the entire length of the coil at once, and not start and stop the process.

Place the coil in the cutting fixture that came with the system. Apply saw blade lubricant on the length of the coil, and then place the blade guide directly above the lubricant. Tighten the blade

guide just until the ends of the guide begin to bend. Using your own rotary power unit recommended by the jump ring maker manufacturer, run the saw over the cutting guide to cut the rings. As you are cutting the length of the guide, press down on the cutting blade holder and maintain even downward pressure. Also when cutting, move the saw assembly in a steady, quick motion the length of the coil. This method gives you the straightest and cleanest cuts for your jump rings.

Remove the jump rings from the cutting fixture and tumble-polish.

Basics
TUMBLING JUMP RINGS

TUMBLING JUMP RINGS

Tumbling is a process for cleaning and polishing jump rings; you can also tumble-polish finished jewelry. I use this method with sterling silver rings, silver-filled rings, gold-filled rings, and colored niobium rings.

The process of tumbling cleans off any oils or tarnish that has collected on the metal. Additionally, you can tumble jewelry with crystals (even with AB coatings), beads, rondelles, and glass pearls. Don't tumble natural pearls or any soft stones, such as turquoise, as they can't withstand the process. Silver items with a patina (such as liver of sulfur) may lose the patina when tumbled. Please be aware of that before tumbling this type of jewelry. If in doubt about the stability of a material or finish, tumble-polish a sample of the item to see how it is affected.

Tumbler Types

Tumblers are basic pieces of electrical equipment that generally consist of a motor and a barrel or bowl that will hold the jump rings and/or finished jewelry. You may have tumbled rocks when you were growing up or with your children. You can use the same type of equipment to tumble jewelry.

With that said, there are two different types of tumblers. What makes the tumblers different is their method of movement.

The first type of tumbler is the rotary tumbler, which is used to tumble rocks. This tumbler has a barrel in which you place your tumbling medium, liquid, and pieces. You then place the barrel on the motor and turn the motor on. The motor causes the barrel to rotate continuously until you turn it off. This tumbler is great for small quantities of jump rings or finished jewelry. It is inexpensive (starting around $80) and readily available at rock shops or discount hardware stores.

The second type of tumbler is the vibratory tumbler, which is the one my husband uses to tumble large quantities of jump rings at one time. It uses a bowl instead of a barrel. The bowl is placed over the motor and when turned on, the motor causes the bowl to vibrate the medium, liquid, and jump rings that you have placed inside. The vibratory tumbler generally costs $150 or more.

Medium and Liquid

The medium used in your tumbler is very important for appropriately cleaning and polishing your pieces. For jewelry, use stainless steel shot. It is important that it is stainless steel. The first time I tumbled some pieces, I used steel shot, and it damaged the jewelry. You can use a "jewelers mix" of stainless steel shot, which is made up of small stainless steel pieces in different shapes and sizes.

You can find stainless steel shot in rock stores or online at jewelry supply stores. It generally takes about two pounds of shot for use in one tumbler. Two pounds of stainless steel shot usually costs about $25–30, but you can use it over and over again if you change the cleaning liquid regularly.

Basics

TUMBLING JUMP RINGS

When tumbling jump rings, place a designated amount of cleaning liquid over the stainless steel shot (medium) in the barrel/bowl. The amount will be specified in the instructions for the tumbler you purchase. Generally, you will cover the shot plus another ½–¾ in. (1.3–1.9cm) with fluid.

The base of the cleaning liquid is water, and you will need to add some type of cleaning agent to the water. In my experience, a citrus dishwashing detergent seems to clean jump rings best. Just like with a front-loading washing machine, you do not want too much bubbling or foam, so two to three drops will be enough.

Another alternative is to use tumbling burnishing fluid. You can find it online at jewelry supply stores. Burnishing fluid usually comes in a concentrate, and you add a prescribed amount to the water you place into the tumbling barrel/bowl. The first time I used burnishing fluid, I did not realize it was concentrated and used too much. This can be expensive, so be sure to read the manufacturer's instructions carefully.

Change the cleaning fluid frequently when you are tumbling pieces. When the cleaning liquid becomes cloudy, you should replace with fresh cleaning liquid. If your tumbled jewelry does not shine when finished, that is also a good reminder that you need to change the cleaning liquid.

Tumbling Process

Place the pieces into the cleaning liquid and push them slightly down into the stainless steel shot. It is best if you can bury them all or partway into the shot. As you tumble, the shot will move around the jewelry along with the cleaning liquid to clean and polish your jewelry.

The time it takes to tumble a piece depends on how much cleaning it needs. For lightly soiled or tarnished jewelry, you may want to tumble for only 3–5 minutes. Heavily tarnished sterling silver pieces may take up to 8 hours or more to return them to their original beauty.

In general, tumble pieces for 6–8 hours to fully polish them. If you are careful that the items you are putting into the tumbler are appropriate for this type of cleaning, you don't have to worry about overdoing it.

Once the pieces have been tumbled, rinse them thoroughly with clear, running water. Dry each piece well. Discard the used cleaning fluid, if necessary, and rinse your shot. Store shot in the barrel/bowl until the next use.

ASPECT RATIO

WIRE GAUGE	WIRE DIAMETER IN MM
14-gauge jump rings	1.63 or 1.6mm
16-gauge jump rings	1.29 or 1.3mm
17-gauge jump rings	1.14 or 1.1mm
18-gauge jump rings	1.02 or 1.0mm
19-gauge jump rings	.912 or .90mm
20-gauge jump rings	.812 or .80mm
21-gauge jump rings	.723 or .71mm
22-gauge jump rings	.644 or .65mm
24-gauge jump rings	.500 or .50mm

GAUGE / MILLIMETERS chart

MILLIMETERS	22	20	18	16	14	12
2.0	◎	◎				
2.25	◎	◎				
2.5	◎	◎	◎			
2.75	◎	◎	◎			
3.0	◎	◎	◎	◎		
3.25		◎	◎	◎		
3.5		◎	◎	◎		
3.75		◎	◎	◎		
4.0		◎	◎	◎	◎	
4.5		◎	◎	◎	◎	
5.0		◎	◎	◎	◎	◎
5.5			◎	◎	◎	◎
6.0			◎	◎	◎	◎
6.5			◎	◎	◎	◎
7.0			◎	◎	◎	◎

Note: Some weaves do not need an aspect ratio calculation to change ring sizes. If the weave is closely woven, you will need to use the aspect ratio to change sizes. Weaves that are loosely woven in very simple weaves may not require aspect ratio calculation to determine alternate ring sizes. You can always try a weave with a ring size you have on hand to see if it works.

ASPECT RATIO

The aspect ratio is the number that represents the relationship between the wire diameter (thickness of the wire from which the jump ring is made, also called the "ring gauge") and the inner diameter (ID) of a particular size jump ring (Ring ID). Please don't let that statement scare you into thinking that we are going into higher math! I will make this very simple for you, so please continue with me.

Most chain mail weaves have a specific size of jump ring (or sizes of rings) that makes the weave turn out beautifully. If the rings are too large, the weave may be loose and sloppy. If the rings are too small, the weave may not work at all, or it may be tight and stiff. In my instructions, I list the rings that work well for each weave. You can use the recommended jump rings, or you can try the piece in a larger or smaller scale.

Aspect ratios are generally in the range of 2.9–7.0. Remember, aspect ratio is not for making a jewelry item longer or shorter, but to make it larger or smaller in scale (a thinner or thicker version). Once you know the gauge and the ring ID that works well in a weave, you can use the aspect ratio calculation to change to another size ring that will also work well in the weave and will make either a more-substantial or a finer-scale version.

Basics

ASPECT RATIO

Aspect Ratio Formula

The aspect ratio (AR) formula is:

$$AR = \frac{Ring\ ID}{Wire\ Diameter}$$

OR   **Ring ID = AR x Wire Diameter**

Before using the formula, to convert the gauge of the wire that was used to make the jump ring into millimeters (mm). The table (p. 9) gives the conversion for different gauges of wire.

Aspect Ratio Calculation Example

Say you have just made a Byzantine bracelet out of 16-gauge 4.5mm ID jump rings. You really love it, but would like to make it in a finer scale—but you don't know what size jump ring would work well and maintain the integrity of the weave. Use your aspect ratio knowledge to figure it out.

First: Figure the aspect ratio of your current bracelet.

$$AR = \frac{4.5mm\ \text{(diameter of the rings you used)}}{1.29\ \text{(16-gauge wire diameter from the table)}}$$

OR

$$AR = \frac{4.5}{1.29}$$

If you do the math, the answer is 3.488 (or round it to 3.5). Therefore, your **AR = 3.5** for a bracelet that uses 16-gauge 4.5mm ID jump rings.

Second: Decide what gauge of jump ring wire you would like to use on your new bracelet.

If you want to make the bracelet smaller in overall scale, you are going to pick 18-gauge. So, using 18-gauge jump rings and an aspect ratio of 3.5 as figured above, the ring ID you would need would be:

Ring ID = 3.5 (AR) x 1.02
(18-gauge wire diameter from table)

OR

Ring ID =3.57 or 3.5 diameter
(I rounded down because 3.5mm is a common size of jump ring)

So, you could use 18-gauge 3.5mm ID jump rings for a finer-scale Byzantine chain bracelet.

Additional Example:

Suppose you wanted to use 21-gauge jump rings for a Byzantine chain to make the overall scale of the bracelet even finer. The equation would be:

Ring ID = 3.5 (AR) x .723 (21-gauge wire diameter from table) **= 2.5mm ID**

You now know that you could make a lovely Byzantine bracelet in 21-gauge 2.5mm ID jump rings.

So: You could confidently make a Byzantine bracelet in 16-gauge 4.5mm ID jump rings, 18-gauge 3.5mm ID jump rings, or 21-gauge 2.5mm ID jump rings.

Examples for You to Calculate

1. What ring ID is needed to make a Byzantine bracelet using 19-gauge jump rings?

2. What if you wanted to make a Half-Persian Bracelet and you were told the AR is 5.5?

(The answers are on the bottom of the page.)

I hope the explanation and examples help make your chain mail experience even more enjoyable, as you gain the freedom to create pieces of jewelry in the size and scale that meets your taste or need.

Project note

All bracelet instructions give jump ring amounts for 7-in. (18cm) length bracelets. I have also included the number of rings per in. (cm) so you can easily adjust the length of the chain as needed. Necklace lengths are noted in their instructions.

Beginner
Weaves

Byzantine and Flowers
Bracelet and Earrings

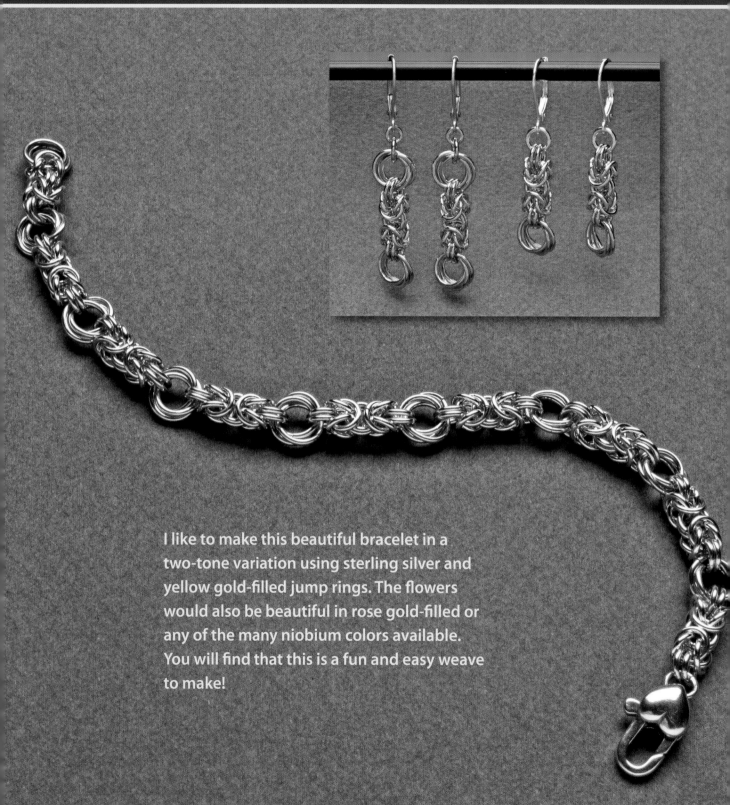

I like to make this beautiful bracelet in a
two-tone variation using sterling silver and
yellow gold-filled jump rings. The flowers
would also be beautiful in rose gold-filled or
any of the many niobium colors available.
You will find that this is a fun and easy weave
to make!

a

b

c

d

e

MATERIALS

Bracelet
- 72 18-gauge 3.5mm ID sterling silver jump rings, 10 rings/in. (4 rings/cm)
- Yellow gold-filled jump rings
  - 54 18-gauge 3.5mm ID (small), 8 rings/in. (3 rings/cm)
  - 24 18-gauge 6.0mm ID (large), 4 rings/in. (1.5 rings/cm)
- Clasp

Earrings (short), 0.75 in. (1.9cm), and (long), 1 in. (2.5cm)
- 18 18-gauge 3.5mm ID sterling silver jump rings
- Yellow gold-filled jump rings
  - 12 18-gauge 3.5mm ID
  - 6 (short) or 12 (long) 18-gauge 6.0mm ID
- Pair of earring findings

Tools
- Chainnose pliers
- Flatnose pliers
- Wire tie or craft wire

Make the Bracelet

1 Open six sterling silver rings, six small (18-gauge 3.5mm) gold-filled rings, and two large (18-gauge 6.0mm) gold-filled rings. Close two sterling silver rings and one large gold-filled ring. This will make the first segment of Byzantine and the first flower. Continue to open and close rings throughout the pattern as needed.

Make a Byzantine Segment

2 With an open small gold-filled ring, pick up two closed sterling silver rings. Close the gold-filled ring. Run another open small gold-filled ring through the two silver rings and close the ring.

Note: This is called running a ring through the same path. I will use this terminology throughout the instructions.

Run a wire tie or piece of craft wire through the two gold rings. Position the rings in the center of the wire, bend the wire in half, and twist the two ends closed. This is a tool to help you hold onto the chain while it is short **(photo a)**.

3 Pick up an open sterling silver ring and run it through the two silver rings. Close the ring. Run another open sterling silver ring through the same path and close the ring. You now have a 2–2–2 chain **(photo b)**.

Note: A string of numbers like 2–2–2 means that you have a chain that is three rows long with two rings in each row. I will describe the chain like this for all of the instructions.

4 Grasp the chain and wire tie in your left hand, and flip the two top rings out to the sides of the chain like bunny ears. (These will be called bunny ears throughout the instructions.) Lift your fingertips away and pin the ears with

your thumb and first finger to the outside of the chain. Push the flipped rings up a little to position them flat against the sides of the chain. Split the top two rings apart **(photo c)**.

Tip: Don't hold the rings too tightly against the chain, as this will make it harder to weave the next two rings.

5 Insert an open small gold-filled ring between and through both of the rings (the bunny ears) beneath them. These are the two rings that you see when you split the top two rings. Close the ring **(photo d)**.

6 Run another small gold-filled ring through the same path and close the ring. This locks the bunny ears rings in their flipped-down position. This ring placement is called "locking the fold in place." The last two gold-filled rings you placed are called the "locking rings" **(photo e)**.

f

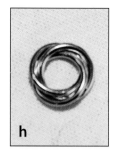

g

h

i

j

k

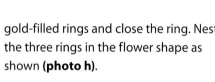

l

7 Scoop up two closed sterling silver rings with an open sterling silver ring and run the open ring through the two rings just added to the chain. Close the ring **(photo f)**. Run a second ring through the same path and close it.

With the chain hanging down, you now have a 2–2–2 chain hanging from the end. This is the signal to go to step 4 and follow the "bunny ears" step again—but first, follow the steps in the Flower Segment below. After that, you will connect the Byzantine and Flower segments together.

Note: If directed to perform the Byzantine Segment steps from these instructions for other projects in this book, do not perform the Flower Segment step.

Make a Flower Segment

8 With an open large gold-filled ring, pick up a closed large gold-filled ring and close the ring. Nest the two rings together as shown **(photo g)**.

9 Run another open large gold-filled ring through the two interlocked gold-filled rings and close the ring. Nest the three rings in the flower shape as shown **(photo h)**.

Connect the Byzantine and Flower Segments

10 Run an open small gold-filled ring through the flower, and before closing, follow steps 4 and 5, using this same small gold-filled ring, to lock the "bunny ears" rings in place. Run a second gold-filled ring through the same path. You will see the small gold-filled rings locking the fold in place and the flower hanging from the gold-filled rings as well **(photo i)**.

Note: The section that you just made would make a short earring: Run an open small sterling silver ring through the two end small gold-filled rings and also through the earring finding. Close the ring. Repeat steps 1–10 plus this note to make a second earring (photo j).

Note: To make a long earring, repeat steps 8 and 9 to form a flower. Remove the wire tie from the end of your current chain. Open the two small gold-filled rings on the end of the chain, run each of the small gold-filled rings through the flower, and close them. Run an open small

sterling silver ring through one of the end flowers and also through the earring finding. Close the ring. Repeat steps 1–10 plus this note for the second earring **(photo k)**.

11 Begin the next Byzantine Segment: Run two small gold-filled rings through the flower and close both rings.

12 Repeat steps 7–10 to complete a second Byzantine and Flower Segment **(photo l)**. Continue across the length of the bracelet until you reach the desired length, ending with a Byzantine Segment. Run a small ring through the end rings of the chain and through one half of the clasp, and close the ring. Repeat on the other end of the chain with the other half of the clasp.

Celtic Rondelle
Bracelet

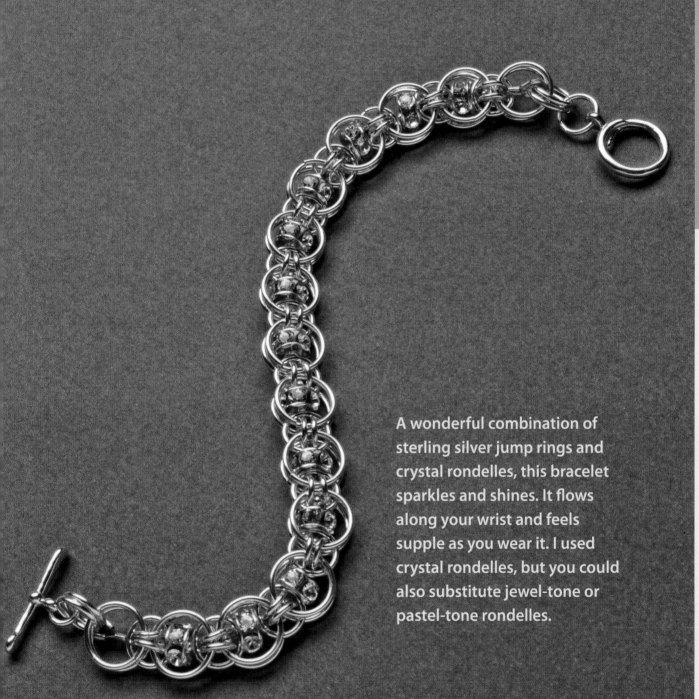

A wonderful combination of sterling silver jump rings and crystal rondelles, this bracelet sparkles and shines. It flows along your wrist and feels supple as you wear it. I used crystal rondelles, but you could also substitute jewel-tone or pastel-tone rondelles.

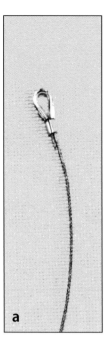

a

b

c

d

e

MATERIALS

Bracelet
- Sterling silver jump rings
  - 30 18-gauge 3.5mm ID, 4 rings/in. (2 rings/cm)
  - 18 18-gauge 6.0mm ID, 2 rings/in. (1 ring/cm)
  - 30 18-gauge 8.0mm ID, 4 rings/in. (2 rings/cm)
- 14 6mm crystal rondelles, 2 rondelles/in.
- 28 2mm sterling silver balls, 2 balls/rondelle
- 15 in. (38cm) fine (0.014mm) beading wire
- 2 sterling silver crimps
- 2 sterling silver wire guards (optional)
- Clasp

Tools
- Chainnose pliers
- Flatnose pliers
- Crimping pliers
- Wire cutters
- Wire tie or craft wire

Add the Wire Guard and Crimp

1 String the beading wire through a crimp, the wire guard, and then back through the crimp. Leave a short piece (1 in./2.5cm or less) and a long piece (remaining wire) extending from the crimp. Make a folded crimp. Trim the short end of the wire; you should have 13–14 in. (33–35.5cm) of beading wire with the wire guard **(photo a)**.

Note: A wire guard is shaped like a horseshoe that has a tube on each end and is open across the top curve. Its purpose is to protect the beading wire from wear by preventing it from rubbing against the jump rings. The inner curve of the horseshoe rubs against the rings instead. You can make the bracelet without the wire guards, but I recommend using them.

Begin the Chain

2 Open a pile of all three sizes of rings. Continue opening rings as needed. Run an open medium ring (18-gauge 6.0mm) through the wire guard and close the ring. Run a second ring through the same path. Run a wire tie through the two closed rings, position them in the middle of the wire, bend the wire in half, and twist the two ends of the wire together **(photo b)**.

3 Run an open large ring (18-gauge 8.0mm) through the two rings on the wire tie and close the ring. Run another open large ring through the same rings on the other side of the wire, and close the ring **(photo c)**.

4 Run an open small ring through the two large rings and close the ring.

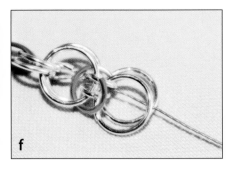

f

g

h

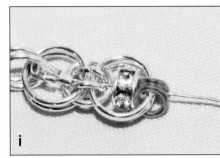

i

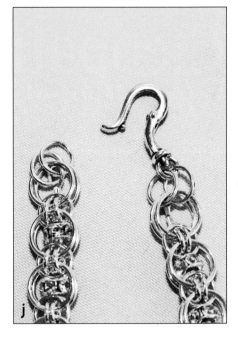

j

Run a second open small ring through the two large rings on the other side of the wire and close the ring **(photo d)**.

5 Run an open large ring through the two small rings and close the ring **(photo e)**. Run a second open large ring through the two small rings on the other side of the wire, and close the ring.

Note: The beading wire always goes through the center of the chain. In every row of two rings, place one ring on one side of the wire and the second ring on the other side.

6 Run an open medium ring between the first set of large rings, around the two small rings, and between the second set of large rings **(photo f)**. Close the ring **(photo g)**.

Note: This medium ring does not go through any rings, but rather goes around and between rings. This is called a floater ring.

7 String a silver ball, a crystal rondelle, and a silver ball onto the beading wire **(photo h)**. Push the ball, rondelle, and ball inside of the large rings.

8 Run an open small ring through the two large rings and close the ring. Run a second small ring through the two large rings on the other side of the wire. Close the ring **(photo i)**. These two small rings will trap the balls and rondelle inside the large rings.

9 Repeat steps 5–8 until the bracelet is the desired length.

10 When you have placed the last set of large rings through the

last set of small rings (step 5), finish off the beading wire with a crimp and wire guard as you did in step 1. Before crimping, be sure that the wire runs fairly loosely through the chain. If pulled tight, the bracelet may be stiff instead of supple on your wrist. When you have crimped the crimp bead, the wire guard should lie within the last set of two large rings. Trim the beading wire tail next to the crimp.

11 Run a medium ring through the two large rings, the wire guard, and the clasp. Close the ring. Run a second medium ring through the same path if the end of the clasp will accommodate it. Close the ring **(photo j)**.

17

Cleopatra
Wired Bracelet

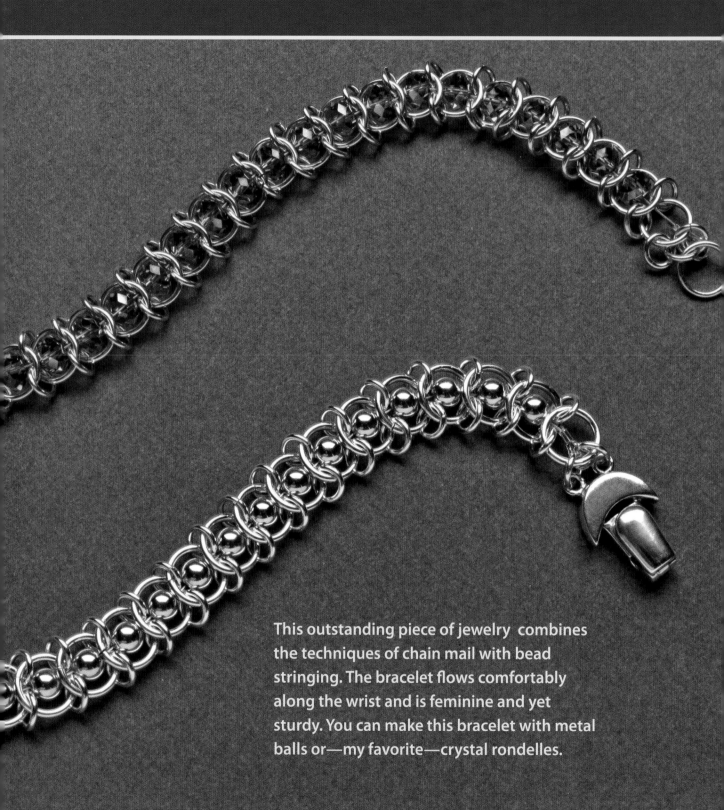

This outstanding piece of jewelry combines the techniques of chain mail with bead stringing. The bracelet flows comfortably along the wrist and is feminine and yet sturdy. You can make this bracelet with metal balls or—my favorite—crystal rondelles.

a

b

c

d

e

MATERIALS

Bracelet

- Sterling silver jump rings
  - 28 18-gauge 6.5mm ID, 4 rings/in. (2 rings/cm)
  - 58 18-gauge 3.5mm ID, 8 rings/in. (4 rings/cm)
- 28 5mm yellow gold-filled balls or 6mm rondelles, 4 balls or rondelles/in. (2 balls or rondelles/cm)
- 15 in. (38cm) fine (0.014mm) beading wire
- 2 crimps
- 2 wire guards (optional)
- Clasp

Tools

- Chainnose pliers
- Flatnose pliers
- Crimping pliers
- Wire cutters
- Wire tie or craft wire

Make the Bracelet

Follow step 1 of "Add the Wire Guard and Crimp," p. 16, from the Celtic Rondelle Bracelet instructions.

Make the Chain

1 Close two large rings and open two small rings. Continue opening and closing rings as needed. Run an open small ring through both of the closed large rings and close the ring. Run a second small ring through the same path. Close the ring **(photo a)**.

2 Flip the second large ring up on top of the first large ring **(photo b)**. Separate the two small rings, and pull the bottom edge of the top large ring down toward the end of the chain **(photo c)**.

3 Close a large ring. Pick up the closed large ring with an open small ring. Before closing the small ring, run it through the large ring at the end of the chain. Close the ring. Run a second small ring through the same path **(photo d)**. Repeat step 2. Run a wire tie or craft wire through the beginning end large ring, bend it in half, and twist the ends shut **(photo e)**.

Note: Notice that the first large ring is under the second large ring. The second large ring is under the third large ring. It is important to continue this layering throughout the length of the bracelet. The new large ring always goes on top of the last large ring in the chain.

4 Repeat steps 2 and 3 across the length of the chain until it's the desired length.

Note: You can begin adding beads or rondelles anytime after you have at least 2 in. (5cm) of chain.

f

g

h

Add Beads or Rondelles

5 Run a small ring through the first large ring and also through the wire guard on the beading wire. Close the ring. Run a second small ring through the same path. Run the beading wire through the shared space of the first and second large rings, while also going between the two small rings connecting the two large rings **(photo f)**. Pull the wire all the way through.

6 Thread a gold ball or rondelle onto the beading wire and push it inside the second large ring. Repeat step 5. The bead/rondelle should sit in the middle of the second large ring **(photo g)**.

7 Continue adding beads or rondelles along the length of the chain until you have one large end ring that does not have a bead in it. Attach the end of the clasp with one small ring to the last large ring on the bracelet. Run a second small ring through the same path. Remove the wire tie and attach the other clasp half. Try the bracelet on to check the fit. The addition of the beads or rondelles can draw the bracelet up, so you may need to adjust the length by removing or adding rings.

8 Once the bracelet is the correct length, open the small ring(s) that attach the clasp to the end of the bracelet, and remove the ring(s) and the clasp. Finish the end of the beading wire with a crimp and wire guard as you did at the beginning of the bracelet. Before crimping, be sure that the wire runs nicely through the length of the bracelet and is not being pulled too tightly.

9 Run an open small ring through the first large ring, through the wire guard, and through the clasp. Close the ring. Run a second small ring through the same path. Close the ring. Attach the other half of the clasp in the same manner **(photo h)**.

Note: Running the second ring through the wire guard sometimes can make the end of the bracelet stiff. You can skip this pass, if you want.

Crazy Byz
Bracelet

"Magically" add beads in a chain mail
weave by trapping them in a cage of rings
along the length of the chain. Glass pearls or
round stones may be used instead of beads.
Whatever you choose will add touches of
color to the bracelet.

a

b

c

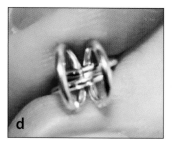

d

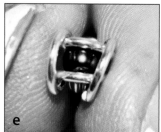

e

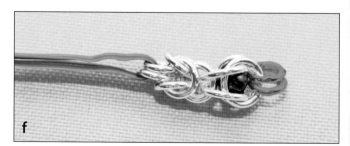

f

MATERIALS

- Sterling silver jump rings
  - 98 18-gauge 3.5mm ID (small), 13 rings/in. (5 rings/cm) plus 10 rings
  - 44 18-gauge 5.0mm ID (large), 6 rings/in. (3 rings/cm)
- 10 4mm beads, glass pearls, or stones
- Clasp

Tools
- Chainnose pliers
- Flatnose pliers
- Wire tie or craft wire

Note: Faceted crystals may not stay within the chain.

Bracelet

1 Open a pile of small and large rings. Continue opening rings as needed. Close two small rings. Run a wire tie or craft wire through the two closed rings, move the rings to the middle of the wire, bend the wire in half, and twist the ends of the wire closed. Run a small ring through the two rings and close. Run a second ring through the same path. Repeat with two more small rings to form a 2–2–2 chain **(photo a).**

2 Follow steps 4–6 in "Make a Byzantine Segment," p. 13, from the Byzantine and Flowers Bracelet and Earrings. Lock the rings in place with two small "locking" rings **(photo b).**

3 Run an open large ring (18-gauge 5.0mm) through the two small rings and close the ring. Run a second large ring through the same path.

4 Run an open large ring through the two large rings on the end of the chain. Run a second large ring through the same path **(photo c).**

5 Holding the chain between your fingers, spread the end two rings apart **(photo d).** Then spread the next two rings apart.

6 Drop a bead down into the cage of rings **(photo e).**

7 Run a small ring through the end two rings of the cage. You may have to move the rings around to position the bead nicely. Close the ring. Run a second small ring through the same path **(photo f).**

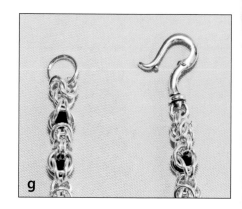

g

8 Run two more small rings through the end small rings and close both rings. Run two more small rings through the end small rings and close both rings. You should now have a 2–2–2 chain made up of small rings. This is your trigger to go to the bunny ears step as you did in step 2, locking the rings in place.

9 Repeat steps 3–8 along the length of the chain until it reaches the desired length. You can end the chain with either a caged section or with a Byzantine section. At the end of the bracelet, run an open small ring through the clasp and the end rings. Close the ring. Remove the wire tie from the other side of the bracelet and with a small open ring, attach the other half of the clasp in the same manner **(photo g).**

Criss-Cross
Bracelets

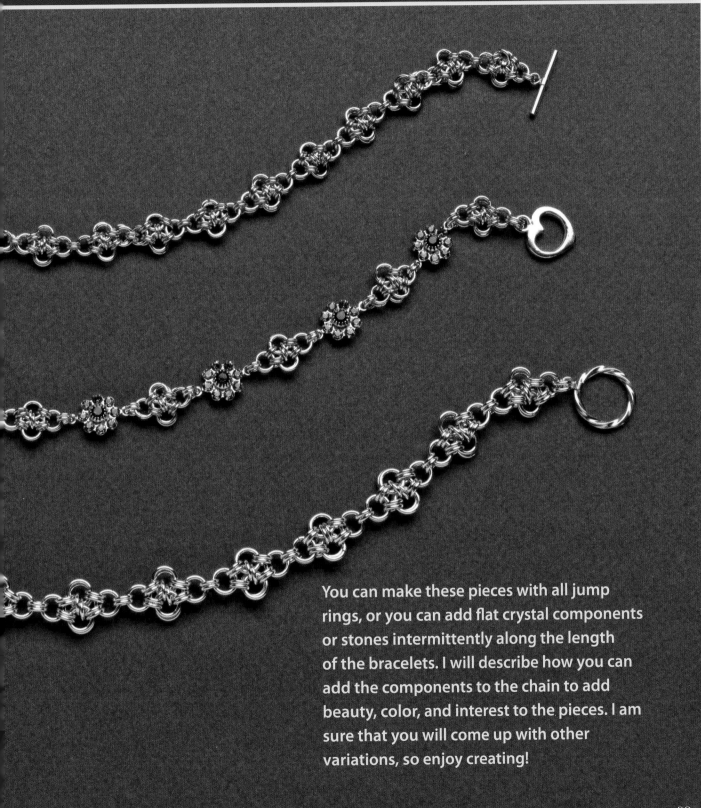

You can make these pieces with all jump rings, or you can add flat crystal components or stones intermittently along the length of the bracelets. I will describe how you can add the components to the chain to add beauty, color, and interest to the pieces. I am sure that you will come up with other variations, so enjoy creating!

MATERIALS

Large bracelet
- Sterling silver jump rings
  - 110 18-gauge 4.0mm ID (large),
    14 rings/in. (5.5 rings/cm) plus 4–10 rings
    for connectors to clasp
  - 100 19-gauge 3.0mm ID (small),
    14 rings/in. (5.5 rings/cm)
- Clasp

Small bracelet (without crystal flower)
- Sterling silver jump rings
  - 140 20-gauge 3.0mm ID (large),
    18 rings/in. (7 rings/cm) plus 4–10 rings
    for connectors to clasp
  - 130 21-gauge 2.5mm ID (small),
    18 rings/in. (7 rings/cm)
- Clasp

Small bracelet (with crystal flower)
- Sterling silver jump rings
  - 90 20-gauge 3.0mm ID (large)
  - 80 21-gauge 2.5mm ID (small)
- 5 double-looped crystal flowers
- Clasp

Note: Use any double-looped flat component. You can also use a drilled flat stone by stringing it on a piece of wire, making a closed or wrapped loop on each end, and attaching as you would any double-looped component.

Tools
- Chainnose pliers
- Flatnose pliers

Note: Each bracelet has two sizes of rings. I will call them large and small. Use whichever is the large and the small for the bracelet you have selected.

a

b

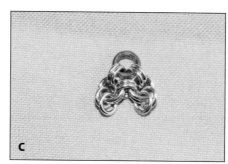

c

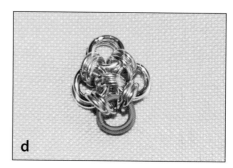

d

Make the Criss-Cross Chain

1 Open a pile of large rings and close a pile of small rings. Continue to open and close rings as needed for the weave. With an open large ring, pick up six closed small rings. Close the ring **(photo a)**. Run another open large ring through the same path and close.

2 With an open large ring, pick up four closed small rings and also run the large ring through two rings already on the first two large rings. Close the rings. Run another open large ring through the same path and close it **(photo b)**.

3 Run an open large ring through two small rings from one pair of large rings and also through the two adjoining small rings from the other large pair of rings **(photo c)**. Run another open large ring through the same path and close it.

4 Repeat step 3 with the four other closed small rings on the large ring pairs. Run a second large ring through the same path. These large rings will now be on the bottom of the criss-cross **(photo d)**.

5 Repeat steps 1–4 to make another criss-cross.

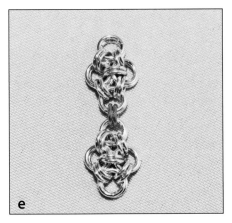

e

f

g

Attach Criss-Crosses for Bracelet without Crystal Flowers

Run an open small ring through the two end rings of one criss-cross and also through the two end rings of a second criss-cross. Close the ring. Run another small ring through the same path (photo e). Continue making criss-crosses and connecting them until the bracelet is the desired length.

Finishing

6 Run a small ring through the end two rings of the end criss-cross and also through the clasp. Close the ring. Repeat on the other end of the bracelet with another small ring and the other half of the clasp. You can double these rings attaching to the clasp if the clasp will accommodate it. You can also add rings to the bar end of a toggle clasp if needed (photo f).

Criss-Cross Bracelet with Flowers

After making at least one criss-cross, run an open small ring through the two end rings of the criss-cross and also through a loop on the end of the crystal flower (or other component piece you have chosen). Close the ring. Attach the other end of the flower component the same way to the end of another criss-cross. Continue alternating criss-crosses with flower crystals until you reach the desired length (photo g). Repeat step 6 to complete the bracelet.

Crystal Dream with a Twist
Bracelet

Twisted rings add texture, while the crystals in colors of your choice add sparkle to this gorgeous bracelet. The sterling silver jump rings add shine to a stunning bracelet.

MATERIALS

- Sterling silver jump rings
  - 42 18-gauge 3.5mm ID, 6 rings/in. (2.5 rings/cm)
  - 21 18-gauge 6.0mm ID twisted, 3 rings/in. (1.25 rings/cm)
  - 21 18-gauge 6.0mm ID, 3 rings/in. (1.25 rings/cm)
- 21 4mm bicone crystals, 3 crystals/in. (2 crystal/cm)
- 15 in. (38cm) fine (0.014mm) beading wire
- 2 sterling silver crimps
- 2 wire guards (optional)
- Clasp

Tools
- Chainnose pliers
- Flatnose pliers
- Wire cutters
- Crimping pliers
- Wire tie or craft wire

a

b

c

Bracelet

1 Follow step 1 of "Add the Wire Guard and Crimp," p. 16, in the Celtic Rondelle Bracelet instructions.

2 Open a pile of rings in each size. Continue to open rings as necessary. Follow step 2 in the Celtic Rondelle Bracelet, using two small rings.

3 Run an open large twisted ring through the two small rings. Close the ring. Run a second large open twisted ring through the two small rings on the other side of the wire. Close the ring **(photo a)**.

Note: The beading wire should always run down the middle of the chain. Always place one ring on one side of the wire and the second ring on the other side of the wire.

4 Run a small open ring through the two large rings on one side of the wire. Close the ring. Run a second open small ring through the two large rings on the other side of the wire. Close the ring **(photo b)**.

5 Run an open large smooth ring through the two small rings on one side of the wire. Close the ring. Run a second open large smooth ring through the two small rings on the other side of the wire. Close the ring.

6 String a crystal on the wire and place it inside the two large rings **(photo c)**.

7 Run an open small ring through the two large rings on one side of the wire and below the crystal. Close the ring. Run another open small ring through the two large rings on the other side of the wire and below the crystal. Close the ring. These rings now trap the crystal inside of the large rings **(photo d)**.

8 Run two open large twisted rings through the two small rings, placing a large ring on each side of the wire. Be sure to keep the small rings below the crystal as you are placing this set of large rings.

9 Continue repeating steps 4–8, alternating smooth and twisted large rings, until you reach the last set of large rings needed for the length of the bracelet.

10 Run a small ring through the last two large rings on the bracelet and through the clasp. This will be placed here temporarily to fit the bracelet to your wrist.

11 Remove the wire tie from the chain. Attach the other half of the clasp to the two small end rings. Repeat with a second ring if the clasp will accommodate a second ring.

12 If the bracelet fits, remove the temporary ring and the small ring from step 10 from the unfinished large end rings. Repeat step 1 to finish the end of the beading wire with a crimp and wire guard. Be sure to check that the wire is supple along the length of the bracelet before you crimp.

13 Run a small ring through the last two large rings, the wire guard, and the clasp. Close the ring. Repeat with a second ring, if desired **(photo e)**.

European Rosette
Bracelet

The European Rosette Bracelet is a variation of the popular European 4-in-1 weave. By adding rings intermittently along the edge of the chain, you develop an edge that looks like rosettes. You could also easily add crystals to the edge rings by stringing a crystal on a headpin and making a wrapped loop to connect the edge ring.

a

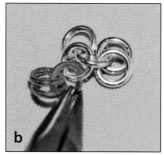

b

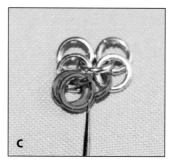

c

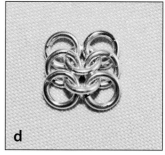

d

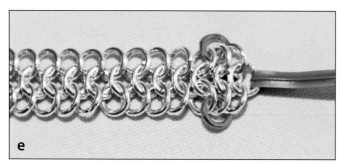

e

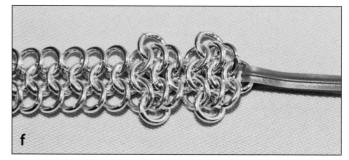

f

MATERIALS

- 176 16-gauge 4.5mm ID sterling silver jump rings, 24 rings/in. (10 rings/cm) plus 4 for clasp connectors
- Clasp

Note: You may also make the bracelet large-scale with 14-gauge 5.5mm ID rings, or small-scale in either 18-gauge 3.5mm ID rings or 21-gauge 2.5mm ID rings.

Tools
- Chainnose pliers
- Flatnose pliers
- Wire tie or craft wire

Make the Bracelet

1 Close four rings and open one ring. Continue to open and close rings as needed throughout the instructions (you will need two closed rings for every one open ring). With the open ring, pick up the four closed rings. Close the ring.

2 Lay the rings in the pattern shown **(photo a)**. Note that the middle ring goes through four rings.

3 With an open ring, pick up two closed rings. Do not close the ring.

4 Run the open ring down through the bottom left side ring of the end three rings on the chain **(photo b)**. Then bring the open ring up through the right side ring of the end three rings on the chain. This is the direction you must thread the rings or the chain will collapse. Close the ring **(photo c)**.

5 Position the rings as shown **(photo d)**. You must always keep the rings layered in this same direction throughout the length of the chain.

6 Repeat steps 3–5 until the chain is the desired length.

7 Lay the chain flat on a beading mat. Run an open ring through three side-by-side edge rings. Close the ring.

8 Repeat step 7 on the other edge of the chain **(photo e)**. You have just made your first rosette.

9 Continue making rosettes by repeating steps 7 and 8 along the

g

length of the chain **(photo f)**. You want a complete rosette on each end, so you may need to add or subtract a row or two.

10 Once you have completed all the rosettes, attach a clasp half with a ring or two on each end of the bracelet **(photo g)**.

Flight of Fancy
Bracelet

I created this weave by combining two classic weaves, Byzantine and Celtic, and adding twisted rings into the chain. This gives interest, texture, and sparkle.

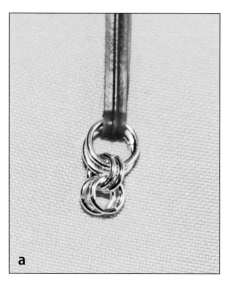

a

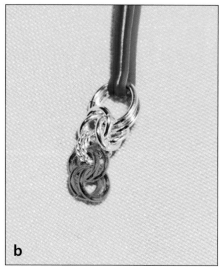

b

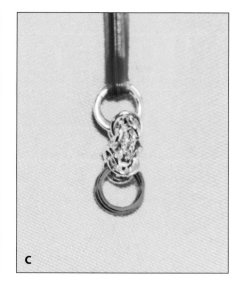

c

MATERIALS

- Sterling silver jump rings
  - 37 18-gauge 6.0mm ID (large),
    5 rings/in. (2 rings/cm)
  - 56 18-gauge 3.5mm ID (small),
    8 rings/in. (3 rings/cm)
  - 28 18-gauge 3.5mm ID twisted,
    4 rings/in. (1.5 rings/cm)
- Clasp

Tools
- Chainnose pliers
- Flatnose pliers
- Wire tie or craft wire

Make a Byzantine Segment

1 Close two large rings and run a wire tie or piece of artistic wire through the rings. Place the rings toward the middle of the wire and twist the ends of the wire closed. Run two small smooth rings through the two large rings to make a 2–2 chain. Run two more small smooth rings through the end small rings to make a 2 (large rings)–2 (small smooth rings)–2 (small smooth rings) chain **(photo a)**.

2 Follow steps 4–6, p. 13, from the Byzantine and Flowers Bracelet and Earrings, using twisted rings as the locking rings.

3 Run a small smooth ring through the two twisted rings. Close the ring. Run a second small smooth ring through the same path and close. You now have a 2–2 chain including the locking (twisted) rings and the two rings you just added. Now run two small smooth rings through the end smooth rings to form a 2 (twisted rings)–2 (small smooth rings)–2 (small smooth rings) chain **(photo b)**.

4 Now you are ready to repeat the bunny ears step (step 2), only this time, use two large rings as the locking rings **(photo c)**. Notice that the twisted rings are in the middle of the chain segment. This is a segment of the Byzantine weave.

Note: For more information about the Byzantine weave, please refer to my first book, *Classic Chain Mail Jewelry*. It contains this weave plus several beautiful variations.

Make a Celtic Segment

5 Run two twisted rings through the two large end rings, and close the rings.

6 Run a large open ring between the two large end rings. Go across and above the twisted rings and out the other side between the two large end rings **(photo d)**. The ring should now be going around the twisted rings and between both sides of the large end rings. It does not go through any rings. Close the ring. This is called the floater ring, as it seems to float between and around other rings, going through none.

7 Run a large open ring through the two twisted rings, staying on top of the floater ring. Close the ring. Turn the chain over and run a large open ring through the two twisted rings on the other side of the floater ring. Close the ring **(photo e)**.

Continue the Chain

8 Run two small smooth rings through the two large end rings and close the rings **(photo f)**.

9 Repeat the Byzantine segment, ignoring the beginning of the chain in step 1 and building a 2–2–2 chain for this step.

10 Repeat the Celtic segment.

11 Continue alternating the Byzantine segments with the Celtic segments until the bracelet is the desired length. It is best to finish the chain at the end of a segment, if possible.

12 Attach a clasp half to the end of the last segment using large or small smooth rings, depending on the clasp. Repeat with the other clasp half on the other end of the bracelet **(photo g)**.

Note: Create a pair of earrings by linking two segments together.

Jeweled Byzantine
Bracelet

The Jeweled Byzantine Bracelet adds
bling to segments of Byzantine chain.
You can have sparkle with crystals, elegance
with pearls, or presence with stones. The
variations in color and combinations are
left up to your imagination.

MATERIALS

Small variation with crystals or pearls
- Sterling silver jump rings
  - 150 18-gauge 3.5mm ID, 14 rings/ segment plus 10 rings for the ends
  - 2 18-gauge 6.5mm ID
- 48 4mm bicone crystals (you may substitute 4mm Swarovski pearls or 12 6mm double-drilled stones)
- 2 12-in. (30.5cm) pieces fine (.014mm) beading wire
- 2 sterling silver crimps
- 2 sterling silver crimp covers (optional)
- Clasp

Large variation with stones
- Sterling silver jump rings
  - 110 16-gauge 4.5mm ID, 14 rings/segment plus 10 rings for the ends
  - 2 16-gauge 8.0mm ID
- 8–9 stones, about ¾ in. (1.4cm) long, with holes drilled about ¼ in. (0.6cm) apart and centered on the stone
- Beading wire, crimps, crimp covers, and clasp as in small variation

Tools
- Chainnose pliers
- Flatnose pliers
- Crimping pliers
- Cutters

Note: Use one stone for every group of four crystals listed in the instructions—you may also use four 6mm crystals across the bracelet or alternate a group of four crystals with a stone between segments.

a

b

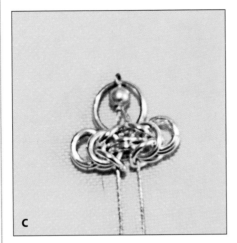

c

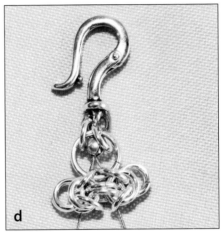

d

Make the Bracelet

1 Build a Byzantine segment with all small rings, following steps 2–6, p. 13, from the Byzantine and Flowers Bracelet and Earrings.

2 Open a large ring and run it through the two rings on the side of the Byzantine segment as shown **(photo a)**. Close the ring.

3 Build a second Byzantine segment as in step 1, and set it aside.

4 String two pieces of beading wire through a crimp, the large ring, and back through the crimp, ensuring that the wires are around the large ring and leaving a short tail. Pull the crimp fairly close to the large ring and crimp the crimp bead.

5 Trim the short tails of the beading wires. Place a crimp cover over the crimp and press it closed (optional) **(photo b)**.

6 Swing the crimp bead toward the middle of the large ring, and run one of the beading wires through the two bunny ears (folded down) rings on both sides of the Byzantine segment. Then run the second beading wire through the other two bunny ears rings on the other end of the Byzantine segment **(photo c)**.

7 Run an open small ring through the large ring and through a clasp half. Close the ring. Run a second small ring through the large ring (on the other side of the beading wire) and also through the clasp. Close the ring **(photo d)**.

e

f

g

8 String two crystals, two pearls or a 6mm stone on one of the beading wires. (If making the large bracelet with the larger stones, run the beading wire through one of the two holes that are drilled through the stone.) String two crystals, two pearls, or a stone on the other beading wire **(photo e)**. (For the large bracelet, run the second wire through the second hole of the stone.)

9 Run each strand of beading wire through the appropriate bunny ears rings on the second segment. Slide the segment against the crystals, pearls, or stone, as shown **(photo f)**.

10 Continue making Byzantine segments, adding beads and sliding the segments onto the beading wire through the bunny ears as in step 9.

11 Once you have reached the desired length of chain, run a large ring through the bunny ears rings on the last segment. Close the ring. Add the clasp half temporarily by running a small ring through the large ring and the clasp half. Close the ring. Add or subtract rings until the bracelet is the desired length.

12 Remove the clasp half from the unfinished end of the bracelet. String the beading wires through a crimp, around the large ring, and back through the crimp. Open the large ring and run it through the beading wire circle on the end of the wire. Crimp the crimp bead. Trim the short tails of the wires. Place a crimp cover over the crimp bead (optional) **(photo g)**.

Note: If you are not able to get the crimping pliers around the crimp when it is on the large ring, open the large ring and remove the circle from it. Being careful not to change the size of the beading wire circle, crimp the crimp closed. Then run a large ring through the beading wire circle and close the ring.

Rolling Byzantine
Bracelet, Necklace, and Earrings

A wonderful variation of the classic Byzantine weave, this chain has extra rolling rings to give it movement and life. You can make the chain all sterling or add rolling rings in another color (yellow gold or rose gold-filled), which is a beautiful contrast. You can also make a necklace in whatever length you want. I am partial to the extra-long necklace.

MATERIALS

Bracelet
- Sterling silver jump rings
  - 144 18-gauge 3.5mm ID (large), 20 rings/in. (8 rings/cm)
  - 43 16-gauge 4.5mm ID (rolling), 6 rings/in. (2.36 rings/cm)
  - 87 20-gauge 2.5mm ID (small), 12 rings/in. (5 rings/cm)
- Clasp

Necklace, 18 in. (46cm)
- Sterling silver jump rings
  - 360 18-gauge 3.5mm ID (large), 20 rings/in. (8 rings/cm)
  - 216 20-gauge 2.5mm ID (small), 12 rings/in. (5 rings/cm)
- 108 16-gauge 4.5mm ID (rolling) gold-filled jump rings, 6 rings/in. (2.36 rings/cm)
- Clasp

Earrings
- Sterling silver jump rings
  - 26 18-gauge 3.5mm ID (large)
  - 12 20-gauge 2.5mm ID (small)
- 6 16-gauge 4.5mm ID (rolling) gold-filled jump rings
- Pair of earring findings

Tools
- Chainnose pliers
- Flatnose pliers
- Craft wire

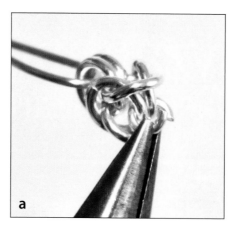

a

b

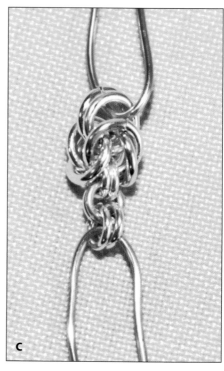

c

Make the Bracelet

1 Follow steps 2–4, p. 13, in the Byzantine and Flowers Bracelet and Earrings, using the large rings. Then perform steps 5 and 6 (the bunny ears step), using small rings as the locking rings. **Photo a** shows how to place the first 20-gauge locking ring.

2 Counting the two small rings as the first set of two rings, form a 2–2–2 chain of small rings **(photo b)**.

3 Use craft wire to stabilize the chain: Form a hook on the end of the wire, making the hook about 1 in. (2.5cm) long. Slip the hook through the end two 20-gauge rings on the chain. The hook wire is at the bottom **(photo c)**.

4 Close three 16-gauge rings. Slip the rings one by one over the wire hook and slide them over the 2–2–2 chain of 20-gauge rings. These are your rolling rings. Be sure to slide the 16-gauge rings over the short end of the hook as the rings move down the wire **(photo d)**.

5 Run an open 18-gauge ring through the end two 20-gauge rings. Close the ring and remove the wire hook. The rolling rings are now trapped on the chain. Run a second 18-gauge ring through the same path and close the ring.

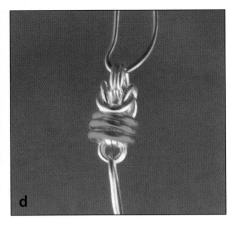

6 Run two 18-gauge rings through the end two 18-gauge rings, closing them as you go. You now have a 2 (small rings)–2 (large rings)–2 (large rings) chain. Perform the bunny ears step as you did earlier, only use 18-gauge rings as the locking rings.

7 Add two more sets of two 18-gauge rings to the end of the chain, for a 2–2–2 chain of 18-gauge rings.

8 Perform the bunny ears step from step 1, only use 20-gauge rings as the locking rings **(photo e)**. Repeat steps 2–8 until the bracelet is the desired length.

9 Run an 18-gauge ring through the end two rings on the chain and through half of the clasp. Repeat on the other end of the chain **(photo f)**.

Make the Necklace
Follow the instructions for the bracelet until the necklace is the desired length.

Note: I also like this pattern in a long necklace without a clasp. Connect the ends of the chain together in the pattern to get a continuous necklace.

Make the Earrings
1 Follow steps 1–6.

2 Run an 18-gauge ring through the last set of locking rings and the earring finding. Close the ring **(photo g).** Repeat to make a second earring.

The Ultimate Chain Mail
Necklace and Earrings

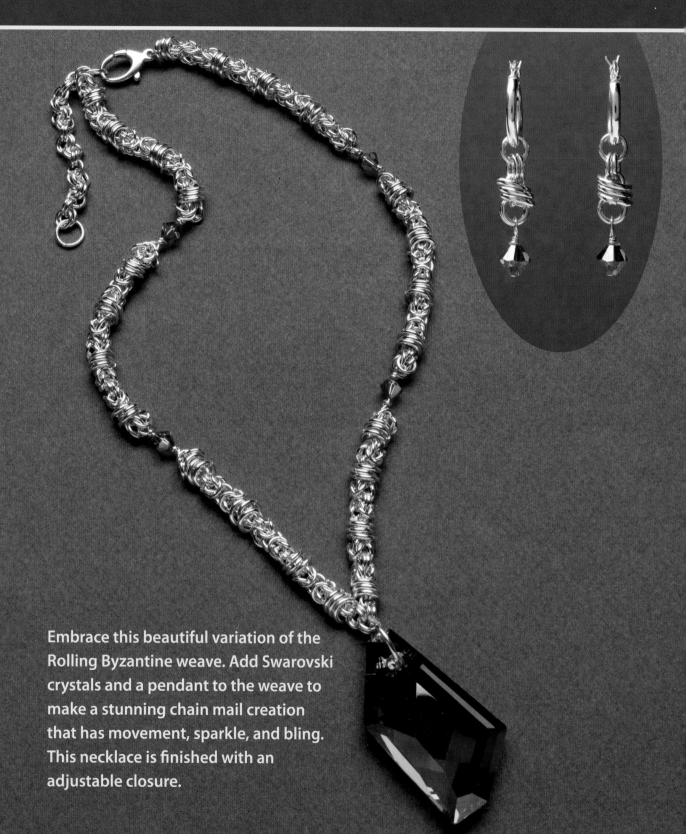

Embrace this beautiful variation of the Rolling Byzantine weave. Add Swarovski crystals and a pendant to the weave to make a stunning chain mail creation that has movement, sparkle, and bling. This necklace is finished with an adjustable closure.

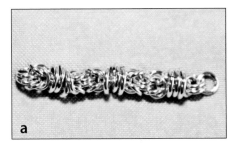

a

b

c

MATERIALS

Necklace, 18 in. (46cm), adjustable to 20 in. (51cm)

- Sterling silver jump rings
  - 250 18-gauge 3.5mm ID
  - 2 18-gauge 6.0mm ID
  - 72 16-gauge 4.5mm ID
  - 16-gauge 10.0mm ID
  - 150 20-gauge 2.5mm ID
- 50mm pendant crystal
- 4 6mm bicone crystals
- 8 in. (20cm) 20-gauge sterling silver wire
- Lobster claw clasp

Earrings

- Sterling silver jump rings
  - 10 18-gauge 3.5mm ID (5 rings/earring)
  - 6 16-gauge 4.5mm ID (3 rings/earring)
  - 8 20-gauge 2.5mm ID (4 rings/earring)
- 2 6mm bicone crystals
- 2 1.5–2 in. (3.8–5cm) 20- or 22-gauge sterling silver headpins
- Pair of earring findings

Tools

- Chainnose pliers
- Flatnose pliers
- Wire cutters
- Roundnose pliers
- Craft wire

Make the Necklace

1 Follow "Make the Bracelet," steps 1–8, p. 39, of the Rolling Byzantine Bracelet, Necklace, and Earrings until you have three sets of rolling rings as shown **(photo a)**. End the chain with two sets of two 18-gauge 3.5mm rings **(photo a,** right).

2 Run an open 6.0mm ring through the end rings on the left end of the chain from step 1. Then build a chain of 3.5mm rings in sets of twos. You will make a chain that has 17 sets of two rings. Run an open 6.0mm ring through the two end rings. Close the ring **(photo b)**.

Note: When using a lobster claw clasp, if you hook the lobster claw clasp on the end ring, the necklace will be 20 in. (51cm). If you hook the clasp on the first large ring, the necklace will be 18 in. (46cm).

3 Working from the right end rings added in step 1, perform the bunny ears step, locking with 20-gauge rings. Add two more sets of 20-gauge rings to the end, forming a 2–2–2 chain of 20-gauge rings. Add three rolling rings and end the chain with two sets of 18-gauge rings. You will now have a chain segment with four sets of rolling rings.

4 On a 2-in. (5cm) piece of sterling silver wire, make the first half of a wrapped loop. Flip the end two rings down as in the bunny ears. Run the open wire loop through the folded rings to lock the fold in place. The wire loop is your locking ring. Make about three wraps with the end of the wire to finish the wrapped loop. String a crystal on the wire. Make another wrapped loop on the other end of the wire.

5 Repeat step 1 above, using the wrapped loop as the beginning ring **(photo c)**. Make a chain segment of four sets of rolling rings off the wrapped loop.

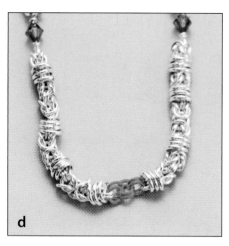

d

e

f

6 Repeat step 3 and 4, only end the four rolling ring chain segment with a 2–2–2 chain of 3.5mm rings as shown **(photo d)**. This is where the pendant will attach.

7 From the end of the 2–2–2 chain, build another four rolling ring chain segment, place a crystal, and repeat until you have two crystals and three rolling ring chain segments on that end of the necklace. Attach the lobster claw clasp to this end of the chain **(photo e)**.

8 Open the 16-gauge 10mm ring and run it through the pendant crystal. Before closing the ring, also run it through the middle rings of the 2–2–2 chain in the middle of the necklace. Close the ring **(photo f)**.

g

Earrings

1 Close two 18-gauge rings. Run a 20-gauge ring through the two rings. Close the ring. Run a second 20-gauge ring through the same path. Add two more 20-gauge rings to the previous two 20-gauge rings so that you have a 2–2–2 chain.

2 Follow steps 3–5 from the Rolling Byzantine Bracelet, Necklace, and Earrings.

3 String a crystal on a headpin and make the first half of a wrapped loop. Run the loop through the two end rings, and complete the wraps.

4 Run an 18-gauge ring through the two end rings and attach to the earring finding of your choice. Close the ring **(photo g)**. Make a second earring.

Zigzag
Bracelet

This bracelet is aptly named, as it seems to zig and zag along your wrist. It is a wonderful charm bracelet base, with a few dozen rings along the edge where you can place charms.

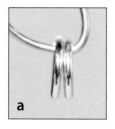

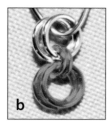

MATERIALS

- Sterling silver jump rings
  - 116 19-gauge 4.0mm ID, 16 rings/in. (6.3 rings/cm)
  - 190 21-gauge 2.5mm ID, 26 rings/in. (10.2 rings/cm)
- Clasp

Tools

- Chainnose pliers, one or two pair for use with small rings
- Flatnose pliers
- Craft wire

Bracelet

1 Open a pile of both sizes of rings. Continue opening and closing rings as you need them. Close two large rings. Run a piece of craft wire through the two rings and twist the end of the wire shut **(photo a)**.

Note: You may want to use two pairs of chainnose pliers when working with the small rings.

2 Run a small open ring through the two large rings. Close the ring. Run a second small ring through the same path. Run an open large ring through the two small rings. Close the ring. Run a second large ring through the same path **(photo b)**. Continue adding rings in a line in this manner until the bracelet is the desired length **(photo c)**. This row of rings is the middle row of your bracelet.

3 Run an open small ring through the top edge of the second set of large rings from the wire end of the middle row of rings. Close the ring. Run a second small ring through the same path.

4 Run an open small ring through the top edge of the third set of large rings from the wire end of the middle row of rings. Close the ring. Run a second small ring through the same path.

5 Run an open large ring through the four small rings you added in steps 3 and 4. Close the large ring. Run a second large ring through the same path **(photo d)**. The two large rings that you just added form the upper row of the chain. You have added them to the middle row of rings you made initially. Please note the triangle that your six small rings form, and also the triangle the three large rings form. You have formed these triangles on the top edge of the chain.

6 Run an open small ring through the bottom edge of the third set of large rings from the wire end of your middle row of rings. Close the ring. Run a second small ring through the same path.

7 Run an open small ring through the bottom edge of the fourth set of large rings from the wire end of the

middle row of rings. Close the ring. Run a second small ring through the same path.

8 Run an open large ring through the four small rings you added in steps 6 and 7. Close the large ring. Run a second large ring through the same path **(photo e)**.

9 Continue across the chain, making alternating triangles of large and small rings above and below on the middle row of rings to form the zigzag pattern.

10 Open the end rings and attach the clasp halves. I added extra rings on the bar end of my toggle clasp so the bar would fit through the toggle end **(photo f)**.

Intermediate
Weaves

Byzantine and Circles
Bracelet

Although big, this bracelet has a light and airy feeling because of the strategically placed larger rings. The weave contains some traits of the Byzantine chain.

a

b

c

d

e

f

MATERIALS

- Sterling silver jump rings
  - 51 19-gauge 7.25mm ID (large), 7 rings/in. (3 rings/cm)
  - 260 18-gauge 3.5mm ID (small), 36 rings/in. (14 rings/cm)
- Clasp

Tools
- Chainnose pliers
- Flatnose pliers

Make the Bracelet

1 Open two small rings and close three large rings. Continue opening and closing rings as you work across the bracelet. Make a large–small–large–small–large ring chain **(photo a)**.

2 Gently pull up on the middle large ring **(photo b)**.

3 Run a small ring through the two small rings in the chain, and close the ring. Be sure it is on top of the large rings **(photo c)**. Turn the chain over and place another small ring through the two small rings on top of the other side of the large ring. Close the small ring.

4 Flip the small ring you just added up toward the top end of the chain. Repeat with the other small ring on the other side of the chain **(photo d)**.

5 Run an open small ring through the two small rings and between the two large rings. Close the ring **(photo e)**.

6 Run an open small ring through the last small ring you added, being sure that the small ring is on top of the two larger rings. Flip the chain over and run an open small ring through the same small ring, on the other sides of the two large rings **(photo f)**.

g

h

i

j

k

l

m

n

7 Run an open small ring through the last two small rings added in step 6 and the large ring next to them. Close the small ring **(photo g).** Add another small ring through the same two small rings, only now go through the large ring on the left of the chain. Close the ring **(photo h).**

8 Run an open large ring through the two small rings just added, being sure to go between the other small rings **(photo i).**

9 Begin to build a Byzantine chain segment off of the large ring on the left. The large ring counts as the beginning two small rings in the Byzantine 2–2–2 chain. The picture shows the two small rings added to the large ring on the left end of the chain **(photo j).** This is the 2–2 of your Byzantine chain; the large ring is the first 2, and the two small rings are the second 2.

10 Add two more small rings to the two small rings you just placed. You now have the Byzantine 2–2–2, only as a 1 large–2 small–2 small rings chain **(photo k).**

11 Flip the two end rings up (bunny ears step). Run a small ring through the bottom end of the two small flipped rings **(photo l).** This is the locking ring; it locks the fold in place. In the traditional Byzantine weave, you would place two rings here, but for this weave, do not.

o

p

q

r

s

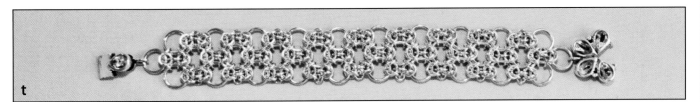

t

12 Run two small rings through the ring just added. Run two more small rings through the two just added **(photo m)**. You now again have a 1–2–2 chain, so it is time to flip the bottom two rings in the bunny ears step.

13 After flipping the end two small rings, run an open large ring as the locking ring as in step 12 **(photo n)**.

14 Repeat steps 9–13 on the large ring on the right end of the chain. You will have a Byzantine segment hanging from each of the outside large rings **(photo o)**.

15 Open the lower center large ring and run it through the two bunny ears rings in the Byzantine segment on the left. Close the ring **(photo p)**.

16 Turn the opening of the large ring you just closed toward the right Byzantine segment. Reopen the large center ring and repeat step 15 on the Byzantine segment on the right side of the chain. Close the ring **(photo q)**.

17 Begin building the middle segment as you did in step 2 at the start of the pattern. Start by placing a small ring to connect the middle large

ring and the bottom right large ring **(photo r)**. Repeat to add a small ring connecting the middle large ring and the bottom left large ring **(photo s)**.

18 Continue working through the pattern, going back to step 3 and repeating along the length of the bracelet. Add a clasp half to the large ring on each end of the bracelet **(photo t)**.

49

Celtic Visions Bracelet

This intermediate weave is fun to make and looks good on your wrist. I especially like it in a two-tone version, as the different sections really stand out.

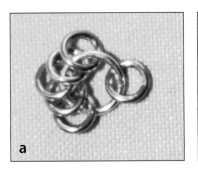

a

b

c

d

MATERIALS

- 58 18-gauge 6.0mm ID sterling silver jump rings, 9 rings/in. (3.5 rings/cm)
- 95 18-gauge 3.5mm ID sterling silver or gold-filled jump rings, 13 rings/in. (5 rings/cm)
- Clasp

Tools
- Chainnose pliers
- Flatnose pliers

Make the Bracelet

1 Open six large rings and close about 20 small rings. Continue opening and closing rings as needed.

2 With a large open ring, pick up six small closed rings **(photo a)**. Arrange them so five rings are clustered together and the sixth ring hangs alone.

3 With another large open ring, pick up five closed small rings. Do not close the ring.

4 Run the large open ring through the single ring from step 2. Close the ring. There will be five loose small rings on each of the two large rings, and they will share a small ring **(photo b)**.

5 Repeat steps 3 and 4 until the chain is the desired length. As you place

rings, the chain will become shorter, so you may need to add more rings later **(photo c)**.

6 Run an open large ring through the four small rings that are stationed around the connecting small ring. Be sure that after you place the large ring, the small rings lie as shown **(photo d)**.

Note: I call these small rings "soldiers" because they are standing at attention. If you go the wrong way through the rings, the soldiers will be lying from right to left and not standing straight. When placing the large ring, think of going in a circle through the small rings. If you start at the top left small ring, you go in from the left, across and through the other small ring from the left to right side (inside to outside).

Hang onto the large ring with the pliers, and let go of the bracelet so it hangs from the large ring. Still holding the large ring, pick the bracelet up and position it so the last two small rings are at the top. Again, go in from the left, across and through the other small ring. Then close the large ring. Check to see if the soldiers are standing at attention. If not, just open the large ring close to the ring that is incorrect and reposition the ring so it stands up straight.

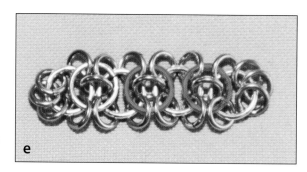

e

7 Repeat step 6 until you have three large rings placed through sets of four small rings **(photo e)**. Now, flip the chain over and repeat step 6 on the other side. You will go through the same sets of small rings that you did on the first side. Once you have a large ring placed on both sides of the chain, you will see the weave **(photos f, g)**.

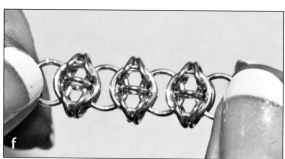

f

8 Continue the chain, repeating steps 6 and 7, until you reach the desired length. You may have to add length to the initial chain, as these steps tend to shorten the bracelet.

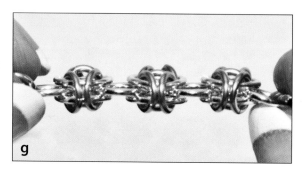

g

9 Remove any small loose rings from the end large ring on each end. Run a small open ring through the end large ring and through half of the clasp. Repeat on the other end. You may need to add some small rings for a toggle clasp **(photo h)**.

h

Camelot
Bracelet

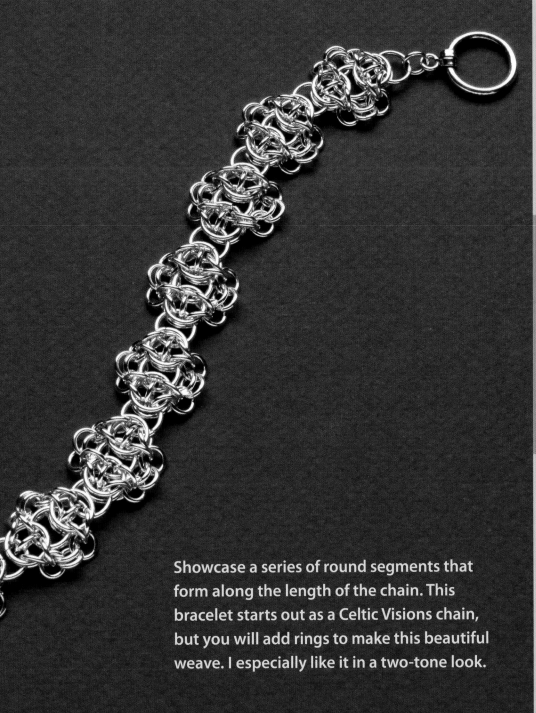

Showcase a series of round segments that form along the length of the chain. This bracelet starts out as a Celtic Visions chain, but you will add rings to make this beautiful weave. I especially like it in a two-tone look.

53

MATERIALS

- Sterling silver jump rings
  - 55 18-gauge 6.0mm ID (large), 8 rings/in. (3 rings/cm)
  - 126 18-gauge 3.5mm ID (medium), 18 rings/in. (7 rings/cm)
  - 36 18-gauge 3.0mm ID (small), 5 rings/in. (2 rings/cm)
- Clasp

Tools
- Chainnose pliers
- Flatnose pliers

Note: **For a two-tone chain, use another color, such as gold-filled, in place of sterling silver for the medium rings.**

Make the Bracelet

1 Follow steps 1–8, p. 51, from the Celtic Visions Bracelet, across the length of the chain until you reach the desired length.

2 Open some small rings. Run an open small ring through the top two rings of a Celtic Vision segment. Close the ring.

3 Repeat step 2 through the bottom two rings of the same Celtic Vision segment. Continue repeating steps 2 and 3 along the top and bottom edges until you reach the end of the chain. I placed four small rings along the top and bottom edge of the chain **(photo a)**.

4 Open some medium rings. Run a medium ring through two adjacent small rings from steps 2 and 3. Run a second medium ring through the same path.

5 Repeat step 4 through the two adjacent small rings at the bottom of the current segment to complete a Camelot segment **(photo b)**.

6 Repeat steps 2–5 across the length of your bracelet. Run an open small ring through the end large ring and half of the clasp **(photo c)**. Close the ring and repeat on the other end with the other half of the clasp.

Note: **Make matching earrings by completing a Camelot segment and attaching it to an earring finding.**

Celtic Zigzag with a Twist
Bracelet

Twisted rings alongside shiny, smooth rings give this variation texture and sparkle. The zigzag effect creates a great deal of interest.

a

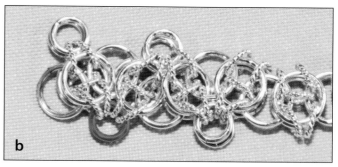

b

MATERIALS

- Sterling silver jump rings
  - 56 18-gauge 6.0mm ID, 8 rings/in. (3.14 rings/cm)
  - 56 18-gauge 4.0mm ID, 8 rings/in. (3.14 rings/cm)
  - 86 18-gauge 3.5mm ID twisted, 12 rings/in. (4.72 rings/cm)
- 2-row clasp

Tools
- Chainnose pliers
- Flatnose pliers

c

Make the Bracelet

1 Follow steps 1–8, p. 51, from the Celtic Visions Bracelet, using twisted rings instead of small rings.

2 Once your chain is the desired length, run a small open smooth ring through two twisted rings on one edge of your chain. Close the ring. Run a second small smooth ring through the same path **(photo a)**.

3 Run a small smooth ring through the next four twisted rings on the opposite edge of the chain, taking two rings from two different sets of large rings. Close the ring. Run a second ring through the same path **(photo b)**. Note how the zigzag is forming.

4 Continue the zigzag pattern across the length of the chain. You may need to add length to the chain, as the zigzag pulls the chain a little shorter. Once the chain is the desired length to fit your wrist, attach a 2-row clasp through the end rings with small rings **(photo c)**.

Celtic Doublet
Bracelet

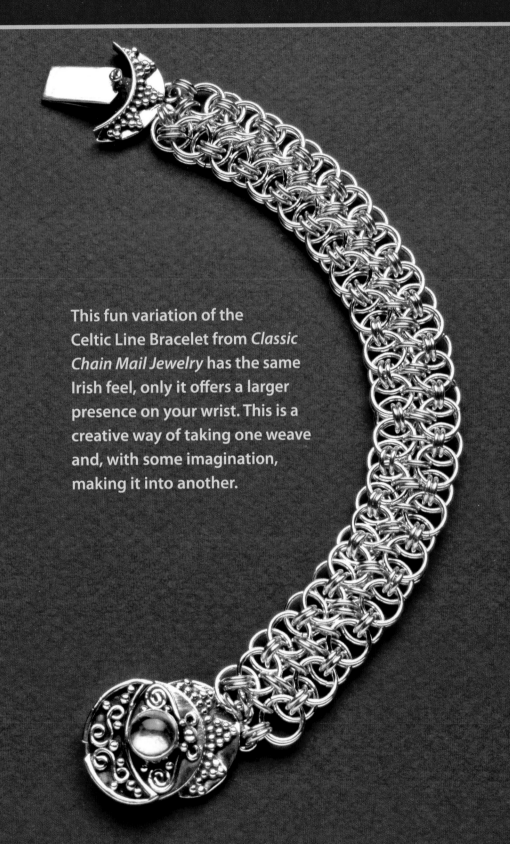

This fun variation of the Celtic Line Bracelet from *Classic Chain Mail Jewelry* has the same Irish feel, only it offers a larger presence on your wrist. This is a creative way of taking one weave and, with some imagination, making it into another.

a

b

c

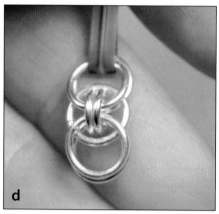

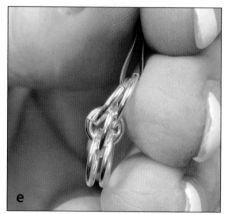

d

e

MATERIALS

- 150 18-gauge 3.5mm ID sterling silver or gold-filled jump rings, 21 rings/in. (8.26 rings/cm)
- 135 18-gauge 6.0mm ID sterling silver jump rings, 19 rings/in. (7.5 rings/cm)
- 2-row clasp

Tools
- Chainnose pliers
- Flatnose pliers
- Wire ties or craft wire

f

Bracelet

1 Close two large rings. Run a wire tie or craft wire through the rings and twist the ends of the wire closed **(photo a)**. Open a pile of small rings and a pile of large rings. Continue opening rings as needed.

2 Run an open small ring through the previous two large rings and close the ring. Run another open small ring through the same path **(photo b)**.

3 Run an open large ring between the two large rings and around the two small rings. Close the ring **(photo c)**.

4 Run an open large ring through the two small end rings, being sure

that the large ring is lying on top of the floater ring **(photo d)**.

5 Turn the chain over and repeat step 4 on the other side of the floater ring. The floater ring is sandwiched between two sets of two large rings **(photo e)**.

6 Repeat steps 2–5 **(photo f)** until the chain is the desired length, ending with step 3.

7 Repeat steps 1–6 to make a second chain of the same length, ending with step 4.

8 Remove the wire ties from the ends of both chains. With the chain that ended with step 3, remove two large

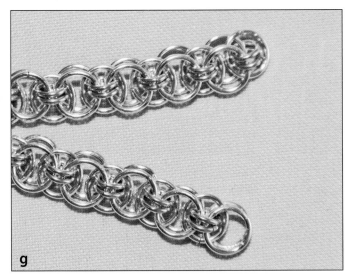

g

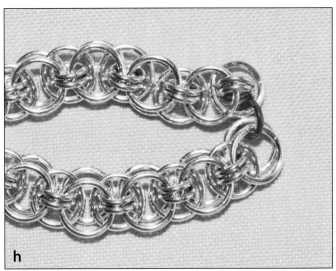

h

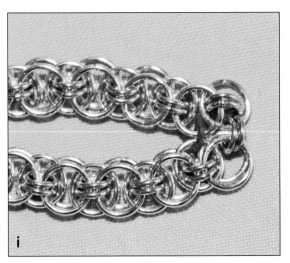

i

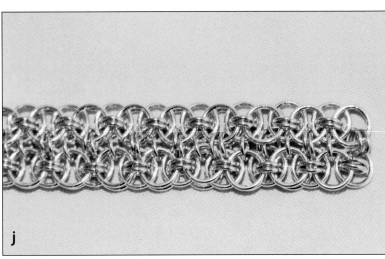

j

rings from the other end of the chain. This chain now has a single floater ring on each end. The other chain has two large rings (step 4) on each end.

9 Lay the two chains side by side **(photo g)**. Run an open small ring through the floater ring on the end of one chain and through the two large rings on the end of the other chain. Close the ring **(photo h)**. Run a second small ring through the same path.

10 Run a small open ring through the next set of large rings in the two chains. This ring will run through a floater ring on one chain and through two large rings on the second chain. Close the ring **(photo i)**. This will be a single ring. You are staggering the chains **(photo j)**.

Note: As you connect the chains, they will shorten. You may find that you need to lengthen them a bit.

11 Once you have connected the chains to the desired length, attach the clasp halves to the end large rings, either directly or with small rings.

Chain Mail Lace
Bracelet, Pendant, and Earrings

Fun to make and comfortable to wear, this weave creates a bracelet that has a large presence on the wrist. At the same time, it is feminine and beautiful, displaying texture, sparkle, and shine. The pendant and earrings complete a beautiful jewelry set.

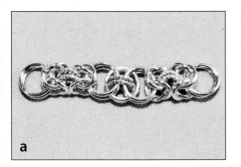

a

b

c

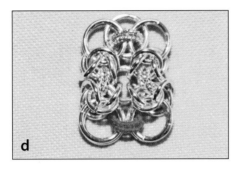

d

e

MATERIALS

Bracelet
- Sterling silver jump rings
  - 100 18-gauge 6.0mm ID (large), 14 rings/in. (5.5 rings/cm)
  - 25 18-gauge 5.0mm ID (medium), 3 rings/in. (1.18 rings/cm)
  - 120 18-gauge 3.5mm ID twisted, 17 rings/in. (6.7 rings/cm)
  - 150 18-gauge 3.5mm ID (small), 20 rings/in. (8 rings/cm)
- 2-row clasp

Pendant
- Sterling silver jump rings
  - 11 16-gauge 7.5mm ID (large)
  - 5 16-gauge 6.0mm ID (medium)
  - 16 16-gauge 5.0mm ID (small)
  - 8 16-gauge 5.0mm ID twisted
  - Neck chain

Earrings
- Sterling silver jump rings
  - 20 20-gauge 5.0m ID (large)
  - 6 20-gauge 4.0mm ID (medium)
  - 32 20-gauge 2.8mm ID (small)
  - 16 20-gauge 2.8mm ID twisted
- Pair of earring findings

Tools
- Chainnose pliers
- Flatnose pliers
- Wire tie or craft wire

Make the Bracelet

1 Byzantine Segment: Make a Byzantine segment following steps 1–4, p. 32, from the Flight of Fancy Bracelet.

2 Celtic Segment: Continue the chain, building a Celtic segment as in the Flight of Fancy Bracelet, steps 5–7.

3 Lace Segment: Continue the chain, building another Byzantine segment as you did in step 1. You now have a chain that is made up of a Byzantine segment–Celtic segment–Byzantine segment **(photo a)**.

4 Remove the wire tie or craft wire from the chain. Bend the chain so a Celtic segment is across the top and the two Byzantine segments are side by side **(photo b)**.

5 In the middle of the Byzantine segments, run a medium ring through the two rings on the edge of the segment. Do not close the ring.

6 Run the open ring through the corresponding rings on the other edge of the chain. Close the ring **(photo c)**.

7 Run two twisted rings through both sets of two large rings on the working (open) end of the Lace segment **(photo d)**. You are now going to make a Celtic segment at the bottom of the Lace segment, mirroring the Celtic segment at the top.

8 Place a floater ring as you did previously in the Celtic segment section, only go between both sets of large double rings and around the one set of twisted rings at the bottom of the Lace segment. Close the ring **(photo e)**. You now have a completed Lace segment.

9 Run a twisted ring through the top two large rings on the top right corner of the Lace segment. Close the ring. Run a second ring through the same path **(photo f)**.

10 Build a 2–2–2 chain as you did previously, starting with 2 (large rings)–2 (small smooth rings)–2 (small smooth rings) **(photo g)**.

11 Perform the bunny ears step, using twisted rings as the locking rings **(photo h)**. (If needed, refer to steps 4–6, p. 13, in the Byzantine and Flowers Bracelet, Necklace, and Earrings.)

12 Build another 2–2–2 chain with the two twisted locking rings as your first set of 2, and then making the other 2–2 out of small smooth rings.

13 Lock the fold in place with two large rings **(photo i)**.

14 Repeat steps 5 and 6 with a medium ring **(photo j)**.

15 Run two twisted rings through both sets of two large rings on the bottom (open end) of the Lace segment **(photo k)**.

16 Repeat steps 9–15, placing floater rings on every other set of twisted rings on the top and bottom edges **(photo l)**. The alternating floater ring placement creates the lace effect.

Attach the Clasp

17 Run a small ring through the two large rings on one end of the last Byzantine segment. Before closing, also run it through one of the two rings on the clasp. Close the ring. Repeat with a second small ring through the other set of large rings, and attach it to the other ring on the clasp. Close the ring. Attach the other half of the clasp in the same way on the other end of the bracelet **(photo m)**.

Make the Pendant

1 Build a Lace segment, following steps 1–8, only use a large ring in steps 5 and 6 instead of a medium ring.

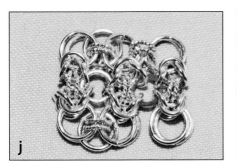

j

k

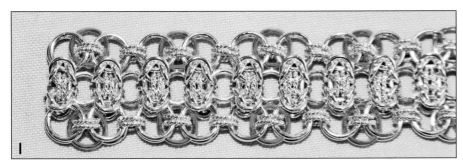

l

m

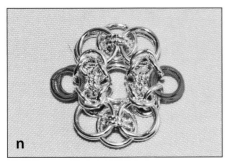

n

o

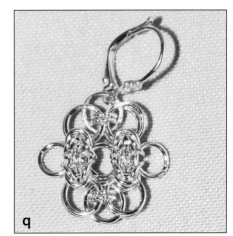

q

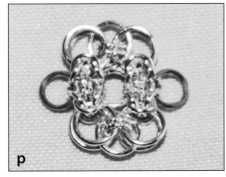

p

2 Run a medium ring through the outside edges of one of the Byzantine segments, as in step 1. Run a second medium ring through the same path. Repeat with two medium rings through the outside edges of the Byzantine segment on the other side of the Lace segment (photo n).

3 Run a small ring through a floater ring and also through the neck chain (photo o).

Make the Earrings

1 Follow step 1 from "Make the Pendant," except use a medium ring instead of a large ring.

2 Follow step 2 from "Make the Pendant," placing only one medium ring on each edge of the Byzantine segment (photo p).

3 Once the Lace segment is complete, open one of the floater rings and run it through an earring finding. Close the ring (photo q). Make a second earring.

River of Mail
Bracelet

Create a river of silver that ripples along your wrist. The combination of smooth and twisted rings adds to the flowing water effect. Your will love this substantial bracelet!

a

b

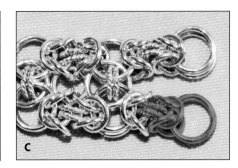

c

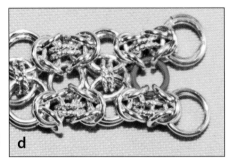

d

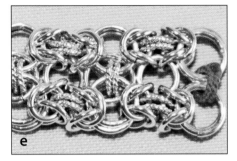

e

f

MATERIALS

- Sterling silver jump rings
  - 56 18-gauge 6.0mm ID (large), 8 rings/in. (3 rings/cm)
  - 14 18-gauge 5.0mm ID (medium), 2 rings/in. (1 ring/cm)
  - 224 18-gauge 3.5mm ID (small), 32 rings/in. (12.6 rings/cm)
  - 84 18-gauge 3.5mm ID twisted, 12 rings/in. (5 rings/cm)
- 2-row clasp

Tools

- Chainnose pliers
- Flatnose pliers
- Wire tie or craft wire

Bracelet

1 Build a Lace segment following steps 1–8, p. 61, of the Chain Mail Lace Bracelet.

2 Turn the Lace segment and run two small rings through the two large rings in the top right corner of the chain **(photo a)**.

3 Build a Byzantine segment off the two small rings as you did in

the Chain Mail Lace Bracelet, placing twisted rings as the middle locking rings, and with large rings on both ends of the Byzantine segment **(photo b)**.

4 Run two small rings through the two large rings at the bottom right corner of the chain. Repeat step 3, building a Byzantine segment off the large rings at the bottom right corner of the chain **(photo c)**.

5 Repeat steps 5 and 6 from the Chain Mail Lace Bracelet, placing a medium ring between the two Byzantine segments **(photo d)**.

6 Build a Celtic segment on the end of the chain, repeating steps 7 and 8 from the Chain Mail Lace Bracelet **(photos e, f)**.

7 Repeat steps 2–6 (only you are not turning the chain segment), continuing the weave across the length of the bracelet. End with a Celtic segment on the each end of the chain.

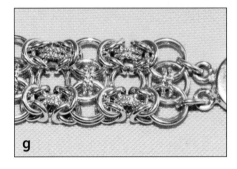

g

8 Run a small ring through two large rings on the end of the chain and one loop on the clasp. Close the ring. Run another small ring through the other two large rings on the end of the chain and the other loop on the clasp. Close the ring **(photo g)**. Repeat on the other end of the chain with the other half of the clasp.

Crystal Mail
Bracelet

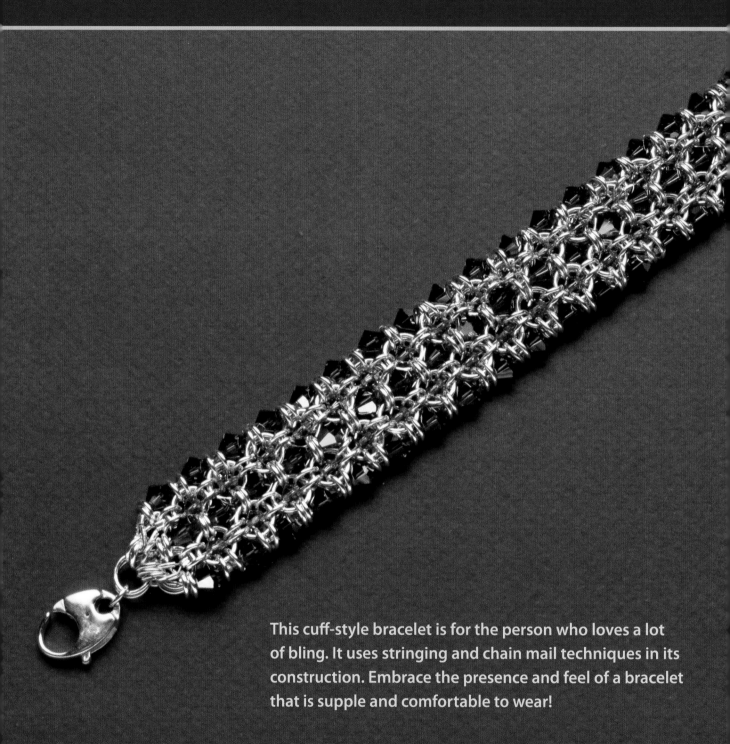

This cuff-style bracelet is for the person who loves a lot of bling. It uses stringing and chain mail techniques in its construction. Embrace the presence and feel of a bracelet that is supple and comfortable to wear!

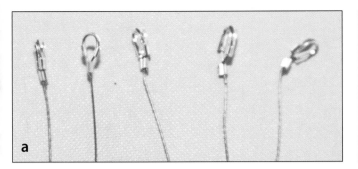

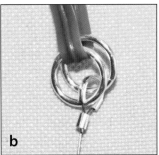

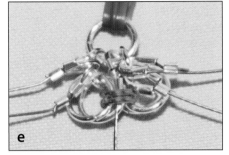

MATERIALS

- Sterling silver jump rings
  - 84 18-gauge 6.0mm ID (large),
    12 rings/in. (5 rings/cm)
  - 105 18-gauge 4.0mm ID (medium),
    15 rings/in. (6 rings/cm)
  - 196 18-gauge 3.5mm ID (small),
    28 rings/in. (11 rings/cm)
- 55 6mm bicone crystals (large)
- 33 4mm bicone crystals (small)
- 75 11º seed beads, silver-lined crystal (or
  other silver color to blend with the rings)
- 5 12-in. (30.5cm) pieces of fine (0.014mm)
  beading wire
- 10 wire guards (optional)
- 10 crimps
- Clasp

Tools
- Chainnose pliers
- Flatnose pliers
- Crimping pliers
- Wire cutters
- Wire tie or craft wire

Bracelet

1 Follow step 1, p. 16, from the Celtic Rondelle Bracelet to secure a wire guard and crimp on the end of a piece of beading wire. Repeat for all five pieces of wire **(photo a)**.

2 Open and run a large ring through the wire guard on one piece of beading wire. Close the ring. Run a second large ring through the same path.

3 Run a wire tie or craft wire through the two rings **(photo b)**. Twist the ends of the wire tie closed.

4 Open a medium ring and close two large rings. With the open ring, pick up two wire guards (with wire attached) and the two closed rings. Run the open ring through the two rings on the wire tie and close the ring **(photo c)**.

5 Repeat step 4, placing the medium ring with the two remaining pieces of beading wire on the other side of the wire guard **(photo d)**.

Note: Place all of the wire guards on the same side of the chain.

6 Open two small rings. Run one of these rings through the four large rings at the bottom of the chain. Close the ring. Run a second ring through the same path. Thread the middle beading wire down through the two rings you just placed **(photo e)**. This is wire number 3.

7 Run four open small rings through two of the large rings that are at the end (or bottom) of your chain **(photo f)**.

8 Repeat step 7, running through the two large rings on the opposite end of the chain **(photo g)**.

9 With an open large ring, pick up six small closed rings. Run the large ring through the inside two small rings on one side of the chain. You placed these small rings in step 7. Close the ring **(photo h)**. Run another large ring through the same path.

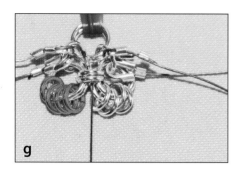

g

h

i

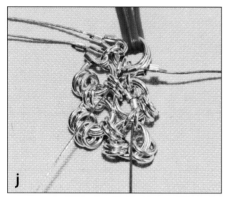

j

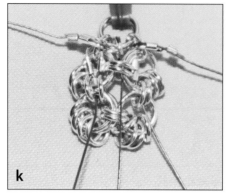

k

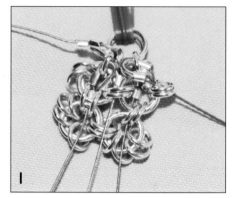

l

10 With an open large ring, pick up four closed small rings. Run the large ring through the inside two small rings from the set of six closed small rings in the last step. Before closing, also run it through the two inside small rings hanging from the large ring above. Close the ring. Run a second large ring through the same path (**photo i**).

Note: In this weave, you will run the beading wire between and sometimes through rings.

11 Run one of the two pieces of beading wire on the right side of your chain down between the two small rings, and at the same time, between the two sets of two large rings that the small rings are going around (**photo j**). This is wire number 4.

12 Repeat step 11 on the left side of the chain (**photo k**). This is wire number 2.

13 Run the loose hanging wire on the right side of the chain down through the two loose small rings hanging from the same side of the chain (**photo l**). This is wire number 5.

14 Repeat step 13 on the other side of the chain with the remaining wire (**photo m**). This is wire number 1.

15 String a large crystal on wire 3. Run the wire through the two small rings below it. This will trap the crystal (**photo n**).

16 String a large crystal on wire 1 and then run the wire through the two small rings hanging loosely on the large ring below to trap this crystal (**photo o**)

17 Repeat step 16 with wire 5 (**photo p**). You have now placed your first row of large crystals.

18 String a small crystal on wire 2 and then run the wire between the two large rings and also between the two small rings hanging below it. This traps the small crystal.

19 Repeat step 18 with wire 4 (**photo q**). You have now placed the first row of small crystals.

20 Pick up six small closed rings with a large open ring and run the large ring through the two small rings hanging from two large rings at the end of the chain (**photo r**). Run another ring through the same path.

21 Repeat step 10 on the other side of the chain (**photo s**).

22 Repeat step 16, stringing two 11º seed beads and a large crystal on wire 1 (**photo t**). You will now always string two seed beads before stringing a large crystal on wires 1 and 5 throughout the rest of the bracelet. These help camouflage the beading wire along the edges of the bracelet.

23 Repeat step 22 on the other side of the chain with wire 5.

24 Add two more small crystals as in steps 18 and 19 (**photo u**).

25 Continue building the chain and adding large and small crystals to the desired length. End the chain as shown (**photo v**).

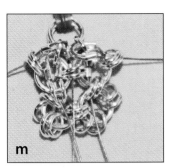

m

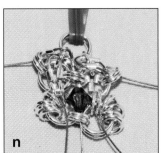

n

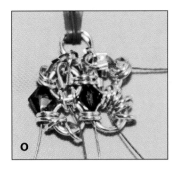

o

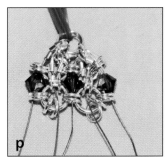

p

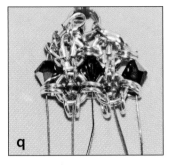

q

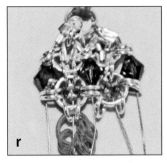

r

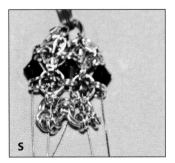

s

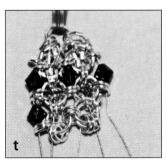

t

u

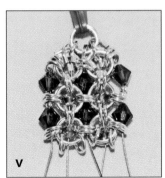

v

w

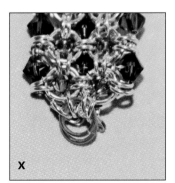

x

26 Temporarily fit the bracelet: Add a small ring through two of the end large rings. Repeat with a small ring through the other two large end rings. Run a large ring through these two small rings and close the ring. Run a small ring through the end large ring and also through half of the clasp. Attach the other clasp half on the other end of the chain in the same way. Fit the bracelet to your wrist—if it is not the right length, add or subtract rings. It is important to fit the bracelet well before crimping the ends of the beading wire, because once crimped, you can't adjust the length. When you have the right fit, remove the temporary rings so the bracelet ends as in step 25.

27 Apply a crimp and a wire guard to the end of each beading wire.

Adjust the tension of the beading wire so that it is not too loose or too stiff. Take some time in this step to get the tension of the bracelet as you want it. Once you are satisfied, crimp the crimp and cut off the short tail. Repeat for all wires **(photo w)**.

28 Run a medium ring through the two end large rings and also through the wire guards on wires 4 and 5. Close the ring.

29 Repeat step 28 with wires 1 and 2.

30 Run a large ring through the rings in step 29, through the wire guard on wire 3, and through the rings in step 28. Close the ring. Run

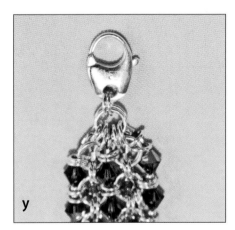

y

another ring through the same path **(photo x)**.

31 Attach a clasp **(photo y)**.

Honeycomb with Bling
Bracelet, Necklace, and Earrings

This set is a beautiful combination of crystals and chain mail. I added twisted rings to the design, which gives more sparkle and texture to the jewelry. They are striking pieces that you will wear for years.

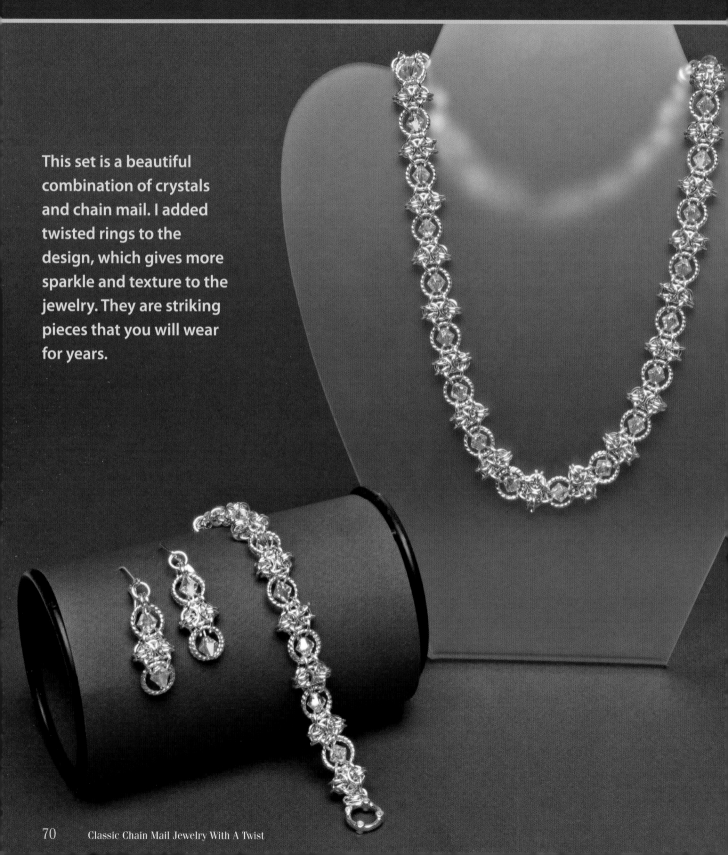

a

b

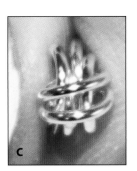

c

d

MATERIALS

Bracelet
- 200 18-gauge 4.0mm ID sterling silver jump rings, 28 rings/in. (11 rings/cm)
- 30 16-gauge 7.5mm ID sterling silver twisted jump rings, 4 rings/in. (2 rings/cm)
- 9 6mm bicone crystals
- 2 crimps
- 2 wire guards (optional)
- 12–15 in. (30–38cm) fine (0.014–0.015mm) beading wire
- Clasp

Necklace, 19 in. (48cm)
- 532 18-gauge 4.0mm ID sterling silver jump rings
- 76 16-gauge 7.5mm ID sterling silver twisted jump rings
- 27 6mm bicone crystals
- 2 crimps
- 2 wire guards (optional)
- 25 in. (63.5cm) fine (0.014–0.015mm) beading wire
- Clasp

Earrings
- 84 18-gauge 4.0mm ID sterling silver jump rings
- 12 16-gauge 7.5mm ID sterling silver twisted jump rings
- 4 6mm bicone crystals
- 2 1.5–2 in. (3.8–5cm) sterling silver headpins
- Pair of earring findings

Tools
- Chainnose pliers
- Flatnose pliers
- Crimping pliers
- Wire cutters
- Wire tie or craft wire

Make the Bracelet and Necklace

Begin the Chain

1 Follow step 1, p. 16, from the Celtic Rondelle Bracelet to place a wire guard and crimp on the end of the beading wire.

2 Open a small (4.0mm) ring and run it through the wire guard. Close the ring. Run a wire tie or craft wire through the ring. Twist the ends closed.

3 Open a small ring and run it through the ring. Close the ring. Repeat with a second small ring, placing it on the other side of the wire guard (**photo a**). Set this section aside for the moment.

Make a Honeycomb Segment Base

4 Run a small open ring through two small closed rings. Close the ring. Run a second small ring through the same path and close the ring. You now have a 2–2 chain.

5 Build a 2–2–2–2–2 chain. This is the base for the honeycomb segment (**photo b**).

e

Attach the Honeycomb Segment

6 Flip two rings down on one end of the honeycomb segment, holding them between your thumb and your first finger (**photo c**). Run a small open ring through the two rings that you just flipped down as shown, and do not close the ring (**photo d**).

7 Run the open ring through the two rings and the wire guard from step 3. Close the ring (**photo e**). I call this a side ring of the honeycomb. This is a difficult step; you are trying to keep the honeycomb segment in position at the same time that you are running the ring through the beginning rings.

8 While holding the honeycomb segment in position, run another small open ring through the same two flipped-down end rings on the other side of the honeycomb segment. This is the other side ring on this end of the honeycomb. Close the ring (**photo f**).

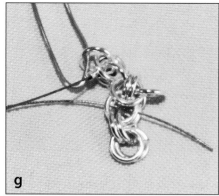

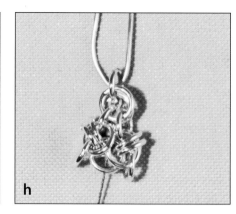

9 Run the beading wire between the center rings of the honeycomb segment base as shown **(photo g)**. Pull it tight.

10 Repeat steps 6–8, adding two side rings on the other end of the honeycomb segment base. Note that you will not run the small ring in step 7 through the wire guard **(photo h)**.

Note: The honeycomb will appear tight, but that is normal for the honeycomb segment on the end of the chain. The rest will lie a bit more loosely.

Make the Twisted Ring Section

11 Run an open twisted ring through the last two side rings added on the honeycomb. Close the ring. Run another twisted ring through the same path, placing it on the other side of the beading wire **(photo i)**. The beading wire will always run down the center of the chain.

12 String a crystal on the beading wire and push it inside the two twisted rings **(photo j)**.

Build the Chain

13 Build another honeycomb segment base.

14 Repeat steps 6–10 to attach the honeycomb segment to the twisted ring section. In steps 7 and 8, run the small rings of the honeycomb segment through the two twisted rings of the twisted ring section **(photo k)**.

Note: When you attach the honeycomb segment to the twisted rings, the crystal becomes trapped in the twisted rings of the chain.

15 Continue building honeycomb segments and twisted ring sections, and connecting them across the length of the bracelet or necklace **(photo l)**.

End the Chain

16 After you have attached what you think is your final honeycomb segment, leave the beading wire alone and temporarily attach half of the clasp. To attach the clasp, run a small

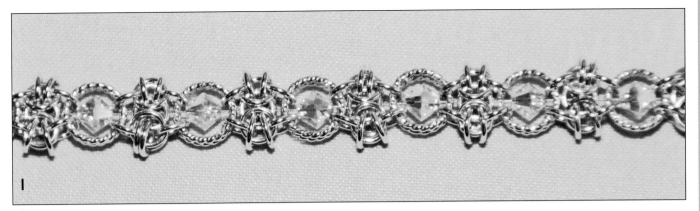

l

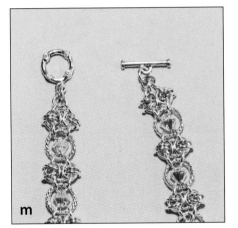

m

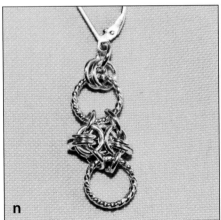

n

o

ring through the two outside side rings on the last honeycomb segment. Then run a small ring through this ring and half of the clasp.

17 Once you are sure of the fit, remove the two rings you added in step 16, thus removing the clasp. Repeat step 1 with this end of the beading wire but before crimping, be sure that your beading wire is not pulled too tightly. If it is, the bracelet will be stiff.

18 Run a small ring through the two outside side rings on the last honeycomb segment. Then run a small ring through this ring and the other half of the clasp **(photo m)**.

Make the Earrings

1 Make a Honeycomb Segment without beading wire. Follow step 6, running the small attachment rings on both sides of the Honeycomb Segment, only do not attach them to anything yet. Run two twisted rings through the two small attachment rings on one side of the segment. Run two twisted rings through the two small attachment rings on the other side of the earring **(photo n)**.

2 String a crystal on a headpin. Run the headpin up through the middle of the honeycomb segment in the same place you ran your beading wire previously, being sure to also go

between the two twisted rings at the bottom and at the top. Then pull the crystal into the inside of the bottom two twisted rings. String a second crystal on the headpin and place it down inside the upper two twisted rings. Shorten the top of the headpin, and pull it down over and/or around one of the twisted rings at the top to form a loop. Run a small ring through the top two twisted rings. Run a second small ring through the two twisted rings on the other side of the attached headpin. Run a small ring through these two small rings and through an earring finding **(photo o)**. Make a second earring.

Wave
Bracelet

Using rings of varying sizes, create a chain that looks like a wave of rings. It is interesting to look at as it lies on your wrist. You will find it to be quite a conversation piece with your friends.

a

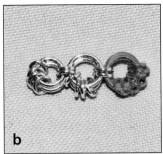

b

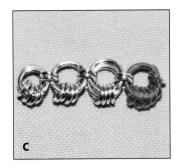

c

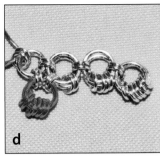

d

e

f

Make the Bracelet
Make the First Row

1 Open two medium rings and close six extra-small rings. With an open medium ring, pick up the six extra-small rings. Close the ring. Run the second open medium ring through the same path. Close the ring.

2 Repeat step 1, substituting large rings for the medium rings. After picking up the six extra-small rings with the first large ring, and before closing it, run the large ring through two of the extra-small rings that are on the medium rings from step 1. Close the ring. Run a second large ring through the same path (**photo a**). Note that the large ring is on the right and the medium ring is on the left.

3 Repeat step 2, only run the large rings through two extra-small rings hanging from the large rings placed in step 2. Be sure that you run through the two extra-small rings on the end of the loose rings so you have four small rings hanging down together from the two large rings (**photo b**). Note that the first large rings have eight extra-small rings on them with two shared with the beginning medium rings and two shared with the second set of large rings. Again, the other four extra-small rings should be hanging together as shown.

4 Repeat step 3, building from the extra-small rings on the last set of large rings in the chain. The rings across the first row will always have eight extra-small rings with the exception of

the first and last rings in the row. See the chain that has three sets of large rings (**photo c**).

5 Place a wire tie or craft wire through the two extra-small rings on the beginning medium rings of the chain, ensuring that the two loose extra-small rings hang down together in the same manner as the four extra-small rings in step 3.

Make the Second Row

6 Open two medium rings and close six extra-small rings. With an open medium ring, pick up the six extra-small rings and, before closing, run the medium ring through two extra-small rings from the first row medium rings and two from the adjacent first row large rings. Close the ring. Run a second medium ring through the same path (**photo d**).

Note: If you have problems running the second medium ring through the same path as the first medium ring, use this alternate method: Run an open medium ring through the two extra-small rings from the first row medium rings and through two extra-small rings from the first row adjacent

large rings. Close the ring. Run a second medium ring through the same path and close. Open six extra-small rings. Run them one at a time through the two medium rings and close. This will give you six extra-small rings hanging from the two medium rings in the same manner as in step 6.

7 Repeat step 6, but run the medium rings through the two extra-small rings from the second row medium rings, two from the first row first large rings, and two from the first row second set of large rings (**photo e**).

8 The second row will continue across the length of the bracelet, repeating step 6. See the chain with a third set of medium rings with extra-small rings added (**photo f**). The second row uses only medium rings with the extra-small rings on them. The first and last sets of medium rings in the second row of the completed bracelet will have 10 extra-small rings, and all other sets of medium rings will have 12 extra-small rings.

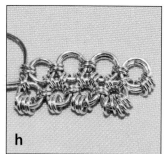

g

h

i

j

Make the Third Row

9 With an open medium ring, pick up four closed extra-small rings. Before closing the ring, run the medium ring through two extra-small rings on the end of the first medium ring in the second row. Close the ring. Run a second medium ring through the same path and close **(photo g)**.

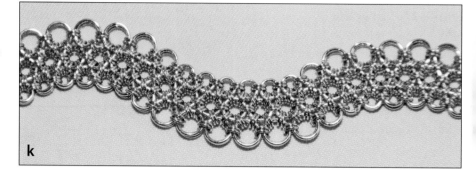

k

10 Run a wire tie or craft wire through the two extra-small rings on the inside edge of the first set of medium rings in the third row **(photo h)**. This will help you keep better track of the position of the chain. You could also now attach your clasp to the extra-small rings on the end instead of running the wire through them **(photo i)**.

11 With an open small ring, pick up two extra-small closed rings and then run the open small ring through two extra-small rings from the first medium ring in the third row, two extra-small rings from the first medium ring in the second row, and two extra-small rings from the second medium ring in the second row. Close the ring. Run a second small ring through the same path and close.

12 With another small ring, pick up two closed extra-small rings and, before closing, run it through two extra-small rings from the first small ring in the third row, two extra-small rings from the second medium ring in the second row, and two extra-small rings from the third medium ring in the

second row. Close the ring. Run a second small ring through the same path and close **(photo j)**.

Build the Bracelet

13 I have given you the directions for building each of the three rows in the chain. When looking at a completed bracelet, you can see that the wave occurs due to the change in ring sizes in a specific sequence in the first and third rows **(photo k)**. The use of extra-small rings (connector rings) stays the same as instructed previously across the bracelet. The large, medium, and small rings (non-connector rings) are the rings that change to cause the wave pattern. Using the connector rings as explained in steps 1–12, use the non-connector rings in sets of two in the sizes as follows:

Row 1: 1 medium–3 large–1 medium– 6 small–1 medium–6 large– 1 medium–6 small–1 medium– 6 large–1 medium

There are eight connector (extra-small) rings on each set of non-connector rings, except for the first and last sets, which will have six rings.

Row 2: 1 medium–1 medium–1 medium-1 medium

This row uses medium rings all across the bracelet. There will be 12 connector (extra-small) rings on each set of non-connector rings, except for the first and last sets, which will have 10 rings.

Row 3: 1 medium–3 small–1 medium– 6 large–1 medium–6 small–1 medium–6 large–1 medium–6 small– 1 medium

There are eight connector (extra-small) rings on each set of non-connector rings, except for the first and last sets, which will have six rings.

14 Connect the clasp to the other end of the bracelet as in step 10.

European 4-in-1
Ring

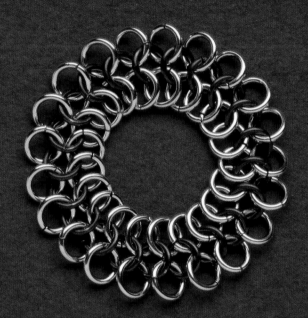

Make a lovely finger ring in any size you desire. It is attractive and very comfortable to wear. You will reach for this one often!

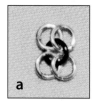

a

b

c

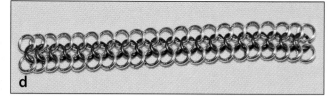

d

MATERIALS
- 75 20-gauge 3.0mm ID sterling silver jump rings

Tools
- Chainnose pliers
- Flatnose pliers
- Wire tie or craft wire

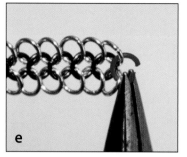

e

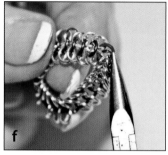

f

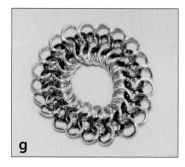

g

Make the Ring

1 Open and close rings as needed throughout the process. Close four rings and open one ring. With the open ring, pick up the four closed rings. Close the ring.

2 Lay the rings in the pattern shown **(photo a)**. Note that the middle ring goes through four rings. This is how the weave gets the name of European 4-in-1 (one ring through four rings).

3 With an open ring, pick up two closed rings but do not close the ring. Run the open ring down through the bottom ring of the end three rings on the chain. Then bring the open ring up through the top ring of the end three rings on the chain **(photo b)**. Close the ring. This is the direction you must always use to place the ring, otherwise the chain will collapse.

4 Flip the rings so they look like the chain shown **(photo c)**. Always keep the rings layered in the same direction throughout the length of the chain.

5 Repeat steps 3 and 4 until the ring is the desired length **(photo d)**. (In the photo, I have turned the chain over so the layering is in the opposite direction). For a size 8 ring, use 20 rows of three rings.

6 Open a ring, and run it through one end of the chain as shown **(photo e)**. Be sure to run it in the same orientation as the middle rings preceding it. Do not close the ring.

7 Run the same open ring through the two rings on the other end of the chain, again keeping the orientation of the ring the same as the middle ring in the working end of the chain. This ring will now have

gone through four rings. Close the ring **(photo f)**.

Notice how the ring flows in an uninterrupted circle once you have closed the final ring **(photo g)**. Try the ring on. If it is too large, remove a middle ring and a row of three rings. Then reconnect the two ends as instructed in steps 6 and 7. If it is too small, remove a middle ring, add another row of three rings, and then reconnect the two ends as in steps 6 and 7. Continue adding or removing rows until the finger ring is the desired size.

Note: If you want to make a two-tone ring, use middle rings in one color and outer rows of rings in another color.

Full-Persian Cross
Pendant and Earrings

These wonderful expressions of faith are challenging but fun to make.

MATERIALS

Pendant
- 48 19-gauge 5.0mm ID sterling silver jump rings
- 12 in. (30cm) 22-gauge sterling silver wire
- Neck chain

Earrings
- 68 22-gauge 3.6mm ID sterling silver jump rings plus connector rings
- 12 in. (30cm) 22-gauge sterling silver wire
- Pair of earring findings

Tools
- Chainnose pliers
- Flatnose pliers
- Wire cutters
- Wire ties or craft wire

Make the Pendant and Earrings

Note: Use the ring size needed for either the pendant or earrings. The weave is the same for both; make two of the earrings and one of the pendant.

1 Open about 20 rings and close two rings. Continue opening and closing rings as needed. Run an open ring through the two closed rings and close the rings. Run a second ring through the same path and close the ring. You now have a 2–2 chain. Run a wire tie or craft wire through two closed rings on one end. Twist the end of the wire shut **(photo a)**.

2 Flip the top two rings down, split the next pair of rings, and place an open ring between the split rings and through the bottom edge of the two flipped rings (which are now on top) **(photo b)**. Run another ring through the same path and close it **(photo c)**.

3 Place a ring through the two rings of the downward-pointing V on one side of the chain. Do not close the ring yet. The pliers are holding the ring you are in the process of placing **(photo d)**.

Note: The downward-pointing V means that the closed end of the V is pointing toward the wire (not the awl in the photo) on the end of your chain. Note that two opposite sides of the chain have a downward-pointing V and the other two sides have an upward-pointing V. You will always place your rings through the downward-pointing V as shown.

4 Before closing, twist the end of the ring upward and go through the top or end rings of the chain **(photo e)**. Close the ring **(photo f)**.

5 Turn the segment over so you see the downward-pointing V on the other side of the chain. Repeat steps 3 and 4 on this side of the chain.

6 Split the top two rings and place an open ring through the two rings in the center of the split rings **(photo g)**. Run a second ring through the same path.

7 Continue the weave until you have used 30 rings **(photo h)**. The top two rings are the bail for the pendant; the neck chain will go through them. This completes the vertical bar of the cross. Note that the front of the bar has the downward-pointing V in front and back.

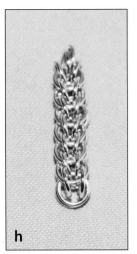

h

i

j

k

l

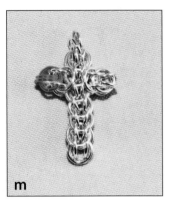

m

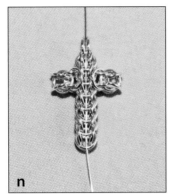

n

o

p

8 Run an open ring through the third set of two side rings of the vertical chain as shown **(photo i)**. Close the ring. Place a second open ring through the next lower set of rings (fourth set from the top) of the vertical chain as shown in the previous photo. Close the ring. Note that these two rings stick out on the right side of the vertical bar.

9 Run an open ring through the two rings just placed. Close the ring. Run a second ring through the same path. Close the ring **(photo j)**.

10 Repeat step 2 **(photo k)**.

11 Repeat steps 3–5 **(photo l)**.

12 Repeat steps 8–11 on the other side of the vertical bar **(photo m)**. Note that the vertical and horizontal bars are rather floppy.

13 Run a piece of 22-gauge sterling silver wire through the vertical bar **(photo n)**. Wrap one end of the wire around a ring close to the end of the vertical bar. Trim the wire to fit the vertical bar, allowing enough to wrap around a ring close to the other end of the vertical bar. You have now supported the vertical bar.

14 Repeat step 13 on the horizontal bar of the cross **(photo o)**. Be sure the end wraps of wire are all on the back of the cross.

Note: If this cross is for the pendant, run the neck chain through the top end rings, which function as a bail. If you used the smaller rings and made earrings, run an open ring through the top two rings of the cross and also through the earring finding. Close the ring (photo p). Make a second cross.

Note: To add some interest to the cross, I like to run a Swarovski crystal headpin through the center of the cross and then loop it to a ring on the back of the cross. This is the red crystal that you see in my completed cross pendant.

Snowflake
Pendant and Earrings

I like to make these pieces in a two-color combination, but you could make the pieces in one color of rings, if desired. For the pendant, add crystals to dangle from the bottom. The earrings are a petite version of the pendant.

MATERIALS

Pendant
- 16 18-gauge 6.0mm ID sterling silver jump rings (large)
- 26 18-gauge 3.5mm ID gold-filled jump rings (medium)
- 10 20-gauge 2.5mm ID gold-filled jump rings (small)
- 2 3mm crystals (optional)
- 2 1–2-in. (2.5–5cm) gold-filled headpins, 22-gauge (optional)
- Neck chain

Earrings
- 32 20-gauge 5.0mm ID sterling silver jump rings (large)
- 52 20-gauge 3.0mm ID gold-filled jump rings (medium)
- 20 21-gauge 2.5mm ID gold-filled jump rings (small)
- 4 3mm crystals (optional)
- 4 1–2-in. (2.5–5cm) gold-filled headpins, 22-gauge (optional)
- Pair of earring findings

Tools
- Chainnose pliers
- Flatnose pliers
- Roundnose pliers
- Wire cutters

a

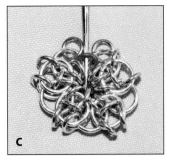

c

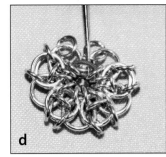

d

b

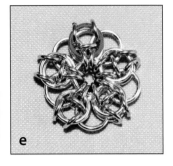

e

f

g

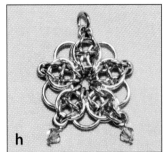

h

Make the Pendant

1 Follow steps 2–5, p. 51, of the Celtic Visions Bracelet, using five large rings and substituting medium rings for the small rings in these steps **(photo a)**.

2 Follow steps 6 and 7 from the Celtic Visions Bracelet, adding four large rings on one side of the chain and four large rings on the opposite side of the chain **(photo b)**. Be sure that one end of the chain has three medium rings running through the end large ring and that there are two medium rings running through the other end large ring.

3 Open the middle ring of the three rings on one end, and connect it between the two loose rings on the other end. Close the ring. The gold ring added is at the top of the circle with an awl through it **(photo c)**. The chain should start to look like the circle in the pendant.

4 Run a large open ring around the center of the circle going through 10 medium rings, two from each grouping. Close the ring. This helps to stabilize the pendant

(photo d). (The awl is under the ring just added.)

5 Place a large ring through the last set of four small rings as in step 6 from the Celtic Visions Bracelet. Close the ring. Flip the pendant over and repeat on the other side **(photo e)**. This gives the pendant five sets of double large rings and five large single rings around the perimeter of the pendant.

6 Run a set of two small gold-filled rings through a set of two medium rings on one of the five points of the snowflake **(photo f)**. See the rings added at the top of the photo. Add two small gold-filled rings at each of the other points of the snowflake.

7 Run an open 18-gauge 3.5mm ring through two of the small rings placed in step 6. This ring is the bail of the pendant **(photo g)**.

8 If you wish to add crystals, string a crystal on a headpin and make a wrapped loop. Repeat with a second crystal and headpin. Open one of the small yellow gold-filled rings on one of the lower points and run it through the wrapped loop. Repeat with the second

i

crystal component, running a small ring from the other lower point on the snowflake **(photo h)**.

Make the Earrings

Follow steps 1–6 of the Pendant, using the correct size of rings for the earrings. Follow step 7, with the 20-gauge 3.0mm ring becoming the connector ring to the earring finding. Run the 20-gauge ring through the two small rings and also through the earring finding **(photo i)**. Follow step 8 to place crystals on the earrings. Make a second earring.

Advanced Weaves

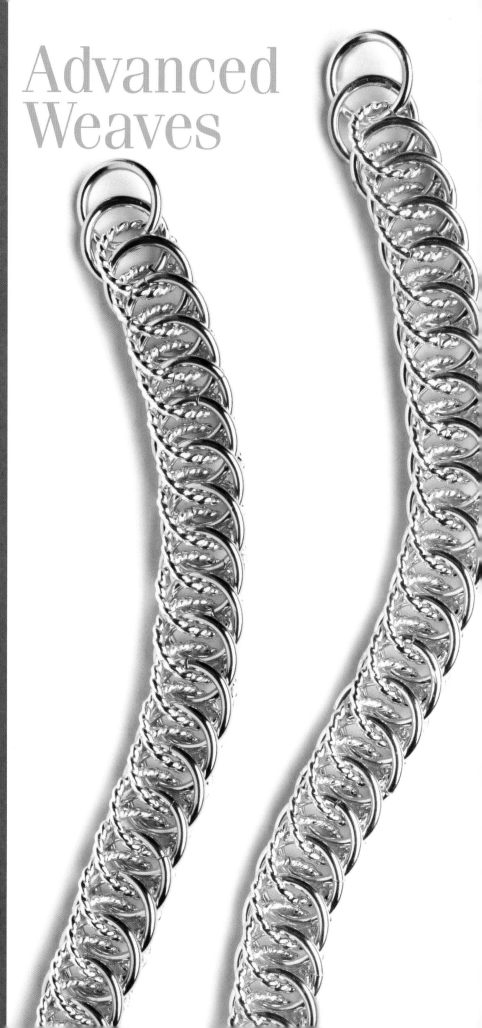

Dragonscale Bracelet

Although it can be a challenge, this cuff-like bracelet is well worth the effort. I recommend that you make your first Dragonscale bracelet two-tone to help you learn the weave. It can be made in two different widths.

 a

 b

 c

 d

 e

 f

 g

 h

 i

MATERIALS

Wide bracelet in sterling silver and gold-filled jump rings
- 280 18-gauge 6.0mm ID sterling silver jump rings, 40 rings/in. (16 rings/cm)
- 280 18-gauge 3.5mm ID yellow gold-filled jump rings, 40 rings/in. (16 rings/cm)
- 2- or 3-row clasp

Wide bracelet in sterling silver and niobium jump rings
- 245 18-gauge 7.0mm ID sterling silver jump rings, 35 rings/in. (14 rings/cm)
- 245 18-gauge 3.5mm ID colored niobium jump rings, 35 rings/in. (14 rings/cm)
- 2- or 3-row clasp

Medium-wide bracelet
- 315 20-gauge 5.0mm ID sterling silver jump rings, 45 rings/in. (18 rings/cm)
- 315 20-gauge 3.0mm ID niobium or gold-filled jump rings, 45 rings/in. (18 rings/cm)
- 2- or 3-row clasp

Tools
- Chainnose pliers
- Flatnose pliers

Make the Bracelet
Set Up the Rings

Note: The setup of the bracelet is the hardest part. Don't get discouraged! Once it is done, you will be repeating four rows, and it will become easier as you go along.

1 Using two small rings and three large rings, connect the rings as shown **(photo a)**. The orientation of the small rings is very important. Be sure the orientation of the rings in the chain always matches the photos.

2 Close two large rings and open three large rings. Lay one closed large ring over one of the small rings in the chain **(photo b)**.

3 Run an open large ring through the small ring that is encircled by the large ring from step 2. Close the ring. This traps the large ring between the other two rows of large rings **(photo c)**.

4 Lay the other closed large ring over the small ring on the other end of the chain as shown **(photo d)**.

5 Repeat step 3 **(photo e)**.

6 Run the next open large ring through the two small rings as shown. This places the ring between the two most recently added large rings **(photo f)**.

Note: In **photo f**, notice the three rows of large rings: a row of three rings at the top, a row of two rings in the middle, and a row of three rings at the bottom. Throughout the rest of the pattern, the large rings will always alternate in a 3–2–3–2 pattern.

7 Open three small rings. Flip the end large ring up and toward the center of the chain. Weave a small ring through the first large ring in the row of two large rings. Be sure the small ring is below the small ring in the row above **(photo g)**.

j

k

l

m

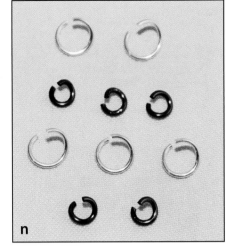

n

8 Flip the large ring back into its original position **(photo h)**.

Note: Be sure the small ring you just added is oriented to the left, below and parallel to the small ring before it as shown in **photo h**. You may have to move it around and tuck it into position. To see if the ring is properly tucked, look at the underside of the chain and see if the small ring appears to be inside the large rings. If the small ring is sticking out between two large rings, pull it into place inside of the large rings.

This is one of the most important steps to perform throughout the weave. If the rings are not properly tucked, the chain will be stiff instead of supple.

9 Run a small ring through both of the sandwiched rings or row of two large rings. Tuck the small ring through the middle large ring of the previous row of three large rings. Again, be sure to tuck this same small ring so that it sits inside of the middle ring of the row of three large rings above it **(photo i)**. Also be sure the newly added small ring is below the last row of two small rings.

10 To complete the row of three small rings, again flip the last large ring toward the center. Run a small ring through the large ring on the end of the row of two large rings **(photo j)**. Flip the large ring back over the small ring. To complete, tuck the small ring inside both the large ring above and the large ring below it **(photo k)**.

Note: There is now a row of two small rings and a row of three small rings.

11 Open two small rings. Run one small ring through the left large ring and the middle large ring from the last row of three large rings. Be sure the small ring stays below the two small rings it is between from the previous row of small rings **(photo l)**.

12 Run the second small ring through the middle large ring and the right end large ring from the last row of three large rings. Close the small ring. Again, be sure the small ring stays below the two small rings it is between from the previous row of small rings **(photo m)**. You have completed another row of two small rings.

Continue the Ongoing Pattern
Open rings and place in the pattern shown. This is important **(photo n)**! These rings represent a row of two large rings, a row of three small rings, a row of three large rings, and a row of two small rings. Always open and lay out your rings in this manner, and only stop during the pattern when you have used all of them. This way, you will always know where you are in the pattern when you begin again. Always end with a row of two small rings and start again with a row of two large rings.

Note: In the Dragonscale weave, you are always adding small rings to the previous row of large rings. Also, you are always adding large rings to the second-to-last row of small rings. Additionally, rows of three rings only connect to rows of two rings, and rows of two rings only connect to rows of three rings.

As I noted at the start of the chain, the large rings alternate between rows of two large rings and three large rings. The small rings also alternate between rows of two small rings and three small rings.

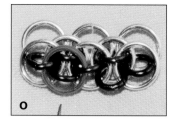

o

p

q

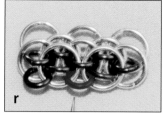

r

s

t

u

v

w

x

y

z

aa

First Row: Two Large Rings

Weave a row of two large rings by running a large ring through the left end and middle small ring from the previous row of three small rings. Close the large ring (**photo o**). Run the second large ring through the middle small ring and the right end small ring from the previous row of three small rings (**photo p**). Be sure the row of two small rings tucks inside the new row of two large rings.

Second Row: Three Small Rings

Weave a row of three small rings through the last row of two large rings (**photos q, r, s**). Again, be sure to keep this row of small rings below the row of two small rings above, and also tuck them inside of the row of three large rings above. **Photo t** shows the back of the chain with the middle blue ring

tucked. Always tuck the ring like this, or the bracelet will be stiff. Correctly tucking the ring will keep the bracelet supple.

Third Row: Three Large Rings

Weave a row of three large rings by running a large ring through the two small rings from above (**photo u**). This places the large ring in the middle of the pattern. Run another large ring through the left end small ring (**photo v**). Then run another large ring through the right end small ring (**photo w**). Be sure to tuck the row of three small rings inside the new row of three large rings.

Fourth Row: Two Small Rings

Weave a row of two small rings by running one small ring through the left end large ring and the middle large ring

in the row of three large rings above (**photo x**). Run the second small ring through the middle large ring and the right end large ring in the row of three large rings above (**photo y**).

Repeat the four rows as above for the rest of the bracelet. At some point, remove the large rings from each end of the first row of large rings. This provides a nice taper to the end (**photo z**). Once you do this, it is easy to tell which end of the bracelet you are working on. When the bracelet is the length you desire, finish off the other end of the bracelet in a taper as well. Attach the clasp to the end rings on the taper point on each end of the bracelet (**photo aa**).

Half-Persian
Bracelet

This advanced weave can be made in two different scales that result in a very nice pair of his-and-hers bracelets. You may want to make your first bracelet in two-tone or with smooth and twisted rings. This will make the weave easier to see as you are learning.

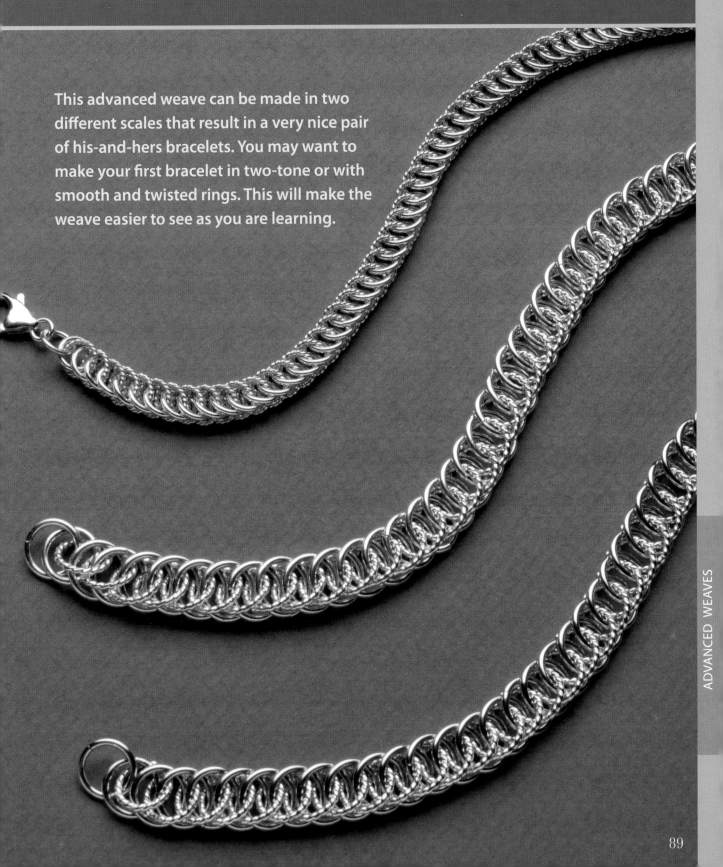

a

b

c

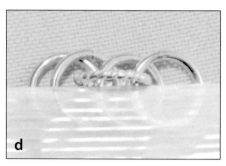

d

e

f

MATERIALS

Large-scale bracelet
- Sterling silver jump rings
  - 42 16-gauge 7.0mm ID, 6 rings/in. (2.5 rings/cm)
  - 42 16-gauge 7.0mm ID twisted, 6 rings/in. (2.5 rings/cm)
  - 4 16-gauge 4.0mm ID, to connect to the clasp
- Clasp

Small-scale bracelet
- Sterling silver jump rings
  - 63 18-gauge 5.0mm ID, 9 rings/in. (3.5 rings/cm)
  - 63 18-gauge 5.0mm ID twisted, 9 rings/in. (3.5 rings/cm)
  - 4 16-gauge 4.0mm ID, to connect to the clasp
- Clasp

Tools
- Chainnose pliers
- Flatnose pliers
- 3–4 in. (8–10cm) strapping tape (standard adhesive tape will not stick well enough)
- Wire tie or craft wire

Make the Bracelet

1 Close four smooth rings and open six twisted rings. Open and close other rings as needed.

2 Lay out the four closed smooth rings from left to right, with the left end ring on the bottom and the subsequent rings layered with the right end ring on top **(photo a)**.

3 Place a piece of the strapping tape over the bottom half of the rings.

4 Place a twisted ring through the hole created by the first and second rings (left to right). Do not close the ring **(photo b)**.

5 Bring the ring around the back and through the hole created by the third and fourth rings (left to right) **(photo c)**. Look closely to see the right end of the twisted ring coming through the hole created by the third and fourth rings. Steps 4 and 5 are probably the most difficult steps in the weave.

6 Close the ring and see how it wove through the four rings **(photo d)**.

7 Place a twisted ring through the hole created by the second and third rings (right to left), being sure to place the ring above the first silver ring. Before closing the ring, run the ring back through the fourth ring (left to right). Close the ring **(photo e)**.

8 Place a smooth ring through the second twisted ring, in front of the fourth smooth ring. Close the ring and note how it lies on top of the previous smooth ring **(photo f)**.

9 Remove the tape carefully **(photo g)**. Hold the beginning piece of chain in your hand in the same position it was on your beading mat.

10 When holding the chain, note that layers of rings are being created **(photo h)**. Always keep the twisted rings toward you, and place the new ring in front of the previously added ring of the same type.

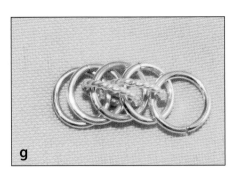

g

h

i

j

k

11 Continue to build the chain by placing a twisted ring through the hole of the second and third smooth rings (right to left) from the end, and then from the back of the chain, taking the ring through the last smooth ring in the chain **(photo i)**. Close the ring. Place a smooth ring through the last twisted ring and close the ring **(photo j)**. You can run a wire tie or craft wire through the end ring as you build the bracelet to help you keep track of the starting end. Repeat this step to the end of the bracelet. End with a twisted ring.

12 When your bracelet has reached the desired length, you may remove the first ring of the chain. Run a 4.0mm ring through the first smooth and twisted rings on the end of the bracelet and one half of the clasp. Close the ring. Repeat on the other end of the bracelet with the other half of the clasp **(photo k)**.

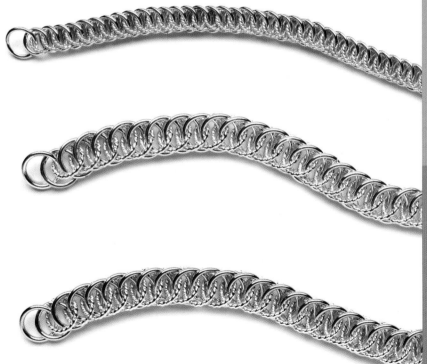

Jens Pind Bracelet

The Jens Pind Bracelet is an advanced weave that makes a wonderful bracelet, necklace, and even an ankle bracelet. It can be made in different scales. I recommend that you make the 16-gauge bracelet first, as these rings are easier to work with than 12-gauge rings. Once you are accomplished in the weave, you can easily use thicker rings to make a bold bracelet for a woman or a great bracelet for a man.

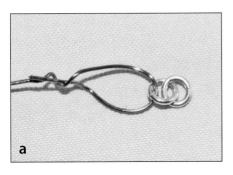

a

b

c

d

e

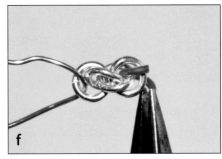

f

MATERIALS

Large bracelet
- 56 12-gauge 5.5mm ID sterling silver jump rings, 8 rings/in. (3 rings/cm)
- Clasp

Small bracelet
- 91 16-gauge 4.0mm ID sterling silver jump rings, 13 rings/in. (5 rings/cm)
- Clasp

Tools
- Two pairs of flatnose pliers or chainnose and flatnose pliers
- Wire tie or craft wire

Make the Bracelet
Begin the Chain

1 Close one ring and open at least a dozen others. You will use all open rings in the weave except for the first one. Slide the closed ring onto a wire tie or piece of craft wire and twist the ends of the wire closed. Run an open ring through the closed ring. Close the ring.

2 Position the two rings as shown **(photo a)**. Pick up the rings with your fingers and position them as shown **(photo b)**. Run an open ring through the shared space of the first two rings. Close the ring. Note the newly placed third ring **(photo c)**.

3 Position the three rings as shown **(photo d)**. Run an open ring through the shared space of the last two rings **(photo e)**. Close the ring.

Note: Throughout the pattern, you will always be running a ring through the last two rings of the chain. The weave is achieved with the proper placement of the ring through the last two rings.

Follow the Pattern Steps

4 Above Step: Place a ring through the last two rings above the third ring from the right end of the chain **(photo f)**. This is the first step in the weave of a repeating set of three steps.

g

h

i

5 Below Step: Place a ring through the last two rings below the third ring from the right end of the chain **(photo g)**. This is the second step.

6 In Front (or On Top) Step: Place a ring through the last two rings in front of (or you might think of it as on top of) the third ring from the right end of the chain **(photo h)**. This is the third step in the weave.

Note: In the row of rings that have edges showing, the first ring lies on top of the ring after it, which lies on top of the next ring in the chain and so on **(photo i)**.

It is important to be able to see how these rings lie. There are four sides to this chain with a row like this on the two sides that are opposite each other. You always want to look at the chain with this row of rings and be sure they are layering on top of each other with the right end ring on the top and the first ring from the left end on the bottom.

Always end with an "in front" step whenever you want to lay your chain down. You will always know to pick up the chain so the last ring is in the "in front" position. You will restart the weave by working the "above," "below," and "in front" steps.

The chain should always be supple. If you find that you have stiff areas, you need to remove rings back to that spot and start again. The stiffness occurred because you placed some rings in the wrong place in the chain. This weave is deceiving because you can place rings in the wrong spot and not see it—but you will feel it.

Attach the Clasp

7 When your chain is the desired length, attach the clasp to the last ring on each end of the chain.

From the Author

I must say that it has been a privilege to have the opportunity to write a second book on chain mail. I have always felt that I am more of a "creator" than a "maintainer," and chain mail has offered me an outlet where I can freely create beautiful pieces of jewelry. By placing what I have learned in books, I can share with others, which gives me a wonderful sense of accomplishment.

As always, I want to thank my family for their love and support. Without them, I would not have been able to write this book. My grandsons, Devon and Logan, have wondered what I have been doing at my computer so much. Their world of wonder has allowed me to better appreciate the things that I see and do.

Steve, my husband, and Megan, my daughter, are both very involved in our chain mail venture. Steve makes the best jump rings in the world (in my opinion), and they are available for purchase from our website, **jewelrybysueonline.com**. Megan has begun developing her own chain mail weaves, which are beautiful. The help and support from both has been invaluable to me in this writing venture.

Most of all, thank you to all of those whose lives I have touched in classes across the country. I appreciate the attempts of the beginners, and have learned techniques and hints from the experienced. Thank you all!

Sue Ripsch shares her chain mail expertise in workshops across the country, and her original designs are represented by a Sedona, Ariz., gallery. She and her husband have developed her passion into an online business, "Jewelry by Sue," through which they offer finished jewelry, kits, and jump rings made to precise specifications. They travel together to many well-known bead, jewelry, and wirework shows to spread their knowledge and appreciation of this fascinating art.

ADVANCED WEAVES

Jump in to more exciting projects!

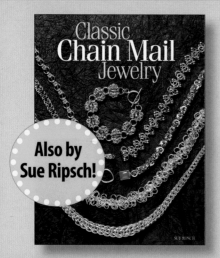

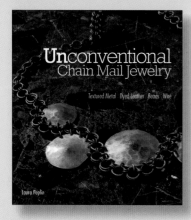